# DECODING UNIVERSAL ENERGY AND HEALING

*- The 4 I's - Healing Methods - Resources*

Donna Linn and Suzan J Wells

Copyright © 2025 Donna Linn and Suzan J Wells.

All rights reserved. No part of this publication may be reproduced, distributed, or transmitted in any form or by any electronic or mechanical means, including information storage and retrieval systems, without a prior written permission from the publisher, except by reviewers, who may quote brief passages in a review, and certain other noncommercial uses permitted by the copyright law.

**ISBN:** Paperback:  978-1-64552-272-0
              Ebook:        978-1-64552-271-3

Lettra Press books may be ordered through booksellers or by contacting:

Lettra Press LLC
30 N Gould St. Suite 4753
Sheridan, WY 82801
1 307-200-3414 | info@lettrapress.com
www.lettrapress.com

Printed in the United States of America

The information, ideas and suggestions in this book are not intended as a substitute for professional medical advice. Before following any suggestions contained in this book, you should consult your personal physician. Neither the authors nor the publisher shall be liable or responsible for any loss or damage allegedly arising as a consequence of your use or application of any information or suggestions in this book.

Because of the dynamic nature of the Internet, any web addresses or links contained in this book may have changed since publication and may no longer be valid. Do we need to say that some only work in US and some work only in England, while many work for both areas.

The views expressed int this work is solely those of the authors and do not necessarily reflect the views of the publisher, and the publisher hereby disclaims any responsibility for them.

# CONTENTS

Forward ................................................................................................ix
Introduction .........................................................................................xi
Ways To Use This Book.................................................................xiv

**Chapter 1    You, Change, and Energy**................................................ 1
    Understanding How Energy Works.......................................... 4

**Chapter 2    An Invisible World**............................................................ 6
    The Four I's........................................................................................11
    Instinct................................................................................................14
    Intention.............................................................................................17
    Intuition..............................................................................................21
    Imagination......................................................................................25
    Navigating the Inner World of You..........................................29

**Chapter 3    About Healing**..................................................................31
    Can I Heal Myself? Do I Need a Healer? .................................33
    You Are Your Own Healer ........................................................ 34

**Chapter 4    Kick-start Your Healing by
              Changing Your Thinking**.................................................35
    1. Willingness to Change .............................................................35
    2. Self-Awareness .........................................................................35
    3. Acceptance ................................................................................35
    4. Forgiveness ................................................................................36
    5. Gratitude ....................................................................................36
    6. Love ..............................................................................................37

**Chapter 5 Twenty-First-Century Healing Modalities:
Articles Contributed by Guest Authors** ....................... 38
Aumakhua-Ki® Energy Balancing & Meditation ............................ 39
Breathwork© ................................................................................. 43
Divine Healing Master Key ............................................................ 49
Esoteric Numerology ..................................................................... 54
Galactic Healing® .......................................................................... 58
Human Design ............................................................................... 62
Mir-Method® ................................................................................. 68
The Essence of Life ........................................................................ 73
The Spiritual Numerology of Moses "Reading your Soul
Integration Maps" ......................................................................... 78
The Stargate Experience ................................................................ 84

**Chapter 6 Twenty-First-Century Healing Modalities:
A Selection of Innovative New Techniques** ............... 89
Anusha Healing ............................................................................. 89
Biologic Decoding® and Biodecoding® ......................................... 90
Celebration of Being ..................................................................... 90
Chios® Energy Healing .................................................................. 91
Eden Energy Medicine .................................................................. 91
Emotional Freedom Technique® (EFT) ......................................... 92
Energy in Motion® (EMO) ............................................................. 92
Men's Groups ................................................................................ 93
Metatronic Healing® ..................................................................... 93
Quantum Touch® .......................................................................... 94
Reconnective Healing®/The Reconnection® ................................ 94
The Body Code® ............................................................................ 95
The Emotion Code® ...................................................................... 95
ThetaHealing™ .............................................................................. 95
Women's Circles ............................................................................ 96

**Chapter 7  Established Healing Modalities:**
**Pre-Twenty-First-Century Healing** .................................97
- Acupressure.................................................................97
- Acupuncture................................................................97
- Affirmations/Positive Thinking ..................................98
- Akashic Records ..........................................................98
- Angels...........................................................................99
- Aromatherapy/Essential Oils.................................. 100
- Astrology ................................................................... 100
- Ayurveda ................................................................... 101
- Color ........................................................................... 101
- Crystals/Gemstones................................................. 102
- Dowsing..................................................................... 102
- Dream Interpretation.............................................. 103
- Family Constellations .............................................. 103
- Feng Shui................................................................... 104
- Flower Essences ....................................................... 104
- Herbs.......................................................................... 105
- Homeopathy ............................................................. 106
- Hypnosis.................................................................... 106
- Kinesiology................................................................ 107
- Magnet Healing ........................................................ 107
- Meditation ................................................................ 108
- Numerology 1-9........................................................ 109
- Nutritional Therapy ................................................. 109
- Past Life..................................................................... 110
- Pendulum.................................................................. 110
- Pranic Healing .......................................................... 111
- Prayer......................................................................... 111
- Pyramid Energy ........................................................ 112
- Reflexology ............................................................... 112
- Reiki ........................................................................... 113

Runes ................................................................................. 113
Sacred Geometry ............................................................. 114
Shadow Work® ................................................................. 114
Shamanic Healing ............................................................ 115
Sound Healing .................................................................. 115
Tarot/Oracle Cards ........................................................... 116
Touch for Health® ............................................................ 117
Traditional Chinese Medicine (TCM) ............................ 117
Vibrational Essences ........................................................ 117

**Chapter 8    Healing with the Body** ................................................ 119
Dance .................................................................................. 119
Grounding/Earthing ......................................................... 119
Massage .............................................................................. 120
Osho Active Meditations ................................................. 120
Qigong/Tai Chi .................................................................. 121
Rolfing® Structural Integration ..................................... 121
Shiatsu ................................................................................ 121
Somatic Experiencing® .................................................... 122
Tantric and Sexual Healing ............................................. 122
Yoga .................................................................................... 123

**Chapter 9    Conclusion** .................................................................. 125

**Chapter 10   Resources** .................................................................. 128

**Chapter 11   New Resources** ......................................................... 157

Acknowledgments ..................................................................... 163
About The Authors .................................................................... 165

# FORWARD

**It has been said, "Living a Life Heals Consciousness, and when Consciousness expresses through Form, it demonstrates the totality of what (its) Source is capable of.**

—Malachite (Channeled by Cé Änn)

Welcome to this moment! A Moment poiised, vibrant and radiant with energetic frequencies magnetizing, manifesting and demonstrating All: You, Thoughts, all that surrounds You - LIFE.

That being stated, you have in your hand (or are viewing/listening), a guide capable of being an ongoing resource and an accomplice to Living your life wholly and consciously with knowledge of modalities known for remedying Body, Mind and Spirit; a virtual cornucopia of the world's known Healing Traditions and some Offerings yet to be fully explored; all presented as opportunities to expand your Healer's Toolbox.

Now you might be saying to yourself, I have no understanding of healing, nor have I considered myself a healer. Good: A great place to start! Consider first that you are indeed a natural born healer. We know this to be true by our Body and how it heals itself without "us" having to do anything! Simply, our Mundane (daily) Mind hasn't a hand in healing though it can definitely get in the way with how it thinks, handles emotions, expresses itself, etc.: this can impede the body's natural (heal) process.

The Awakened (aware) Mind realizes how it participates in the Body's process, and can recognize the mundane mind has impaired or stalled the natural biomechanics and "dis-ease" manifests. Truly, by the time dis-ease manifests, the Body has long been at its healing diagnostics with its innate intelligence - you know this, though it may not always be evident. Practicing with what's laid out before you will achieve a conscious relationship with the Awakened Mind.

Obviously, you've been guided to this resource and the authors Donna and Suzan have a gift waiting for you, by acknowledging the Healer you are and awakening further to useful tools which can assist body and mind. Peruse the table of contents, flip the pages, read the titled sections; who knows what will jump out or trigger an interest to delve deeper into your natural talent.

"Healer, Heal Thyself" right?

Your journey begins here and now…which modality excites you?

Peace on your Path,<br>
Cé Änn,<br>
Sedona, AZ

# INTRODUCTION

At this time, there is much upheaval politically, geographically and personally. The world is being shaken to its core, challenging fundamental beliefs and ways of being. Old ways are crumbling. Many feel a deeper need to understand more about life and its purpose. It is time for global change and new. more positive, ways of living.

We believe that the knowledge and answers sought by many are available from the world of energy. It is invisible, powerful, and offers great potential. This energy has always been there, always will; yet it is continually changing and evolving.

In the past few years, those sensitive to energy have felt its intensity increase. Many have experienced that change is now easier quicker and requires less effort than in recent memory. You have the option to embrace this world of energy to make positive and lasting changes in your life.

We have seen a gradual resurgence of interest in established ways of using energy for healing, creating well-being and positive change. In addition, new and exciting modalities continue to come into the public arena, some integrating established methods, and others bringing in new energies. They all catalyze change in an individual's energy. This may be at a physical, mental, emotional, and/or spiritual level, conscious or unconscious.

Within the realm of energy and healing lies great potential and possibilities to use this energy is innate (natural) but, perhaps, forgotten. However, something is stirring on an individual and global level. Many are searching without knowing what they seek.

Our deepest belief, understanding, and experience tells us what we are truly seeking. You have within you all you need to know. Possibilities are available now that are not yet within mainstream knowledge or in the mass media. Once you start, things will come into your awareness. We invite the part of you that is gently awakening, or perhaps looking for something new, to explore the ideas in this book.

***Decoding Universal Energy and Healing*** introduces you to this world. It can help you navigate the journey of life, reach your full potential, and fulfill your deepest desires. We show you the tools that you already have and can further develop to increase your awareness and empower you to be in the driver's seat of your life.

We share ways to connect with the world of invisible energy, to develop awareness, familiarity, and confidence in life choices and direction. New ideas and possibilities are available for you to explore twenty-first-century healing modalities, established healing modalities, healing with the body, and a resource section of podcasts, websites and books. Whatever technique you choose, it is important to support the body with nutrition and bodywork.

When choosing you can consider whether you prefer:

- Healing yourself or practitioner-led session(s)
- Using s hands-on or hands-off method
- Learning a modality for self-healing and/or giving to others
- Starting with an established modality
- Exploring the newer types of healing
- Accessing healing through the body or with nutrition
- Joining a group or an individual session

- Readings that may give insight and direction—Astrology, Human Design, Tarot, etc.
- Kick-starting your healing with a six-step personal-development approach

Rather than telling you the right way forward, it is our intention offer many options to whet your appetite, plant a seed, or catalyze the change needed for you to start or continue moving toward your new way of being. No one method is best; it is a matter of which one is right for you at each moment. Let yourself be guided by the inner world of your intuition, feelings, senses, and inner knowing(s).

Because of the vastness and ever-increasing new types of energy healing, this is not a comprehensive or exhaustive list. Rather, it is our desire to spark your interest. Allow your inner world to guide you in the right direction.

> **Once you start looking, a whole new world opens up.**
> **Enjoy the scenery. Have fun.**
> **Everything is part of the adventure.**
> **There is no time restriction.**
> **Everything is part of the adventure.**

# WAYS TO USE THIS BOOK

There are many ways to use this book. You may select any of the following options, or find your own way:

- Read parts 1 through 4, and/or dip in and out of other sections
- Open the book at random
- Select a topic from the contents
- Flip through the pages; stop where you feel guided or your eyes are drawn
- Read from cover to cover

Wherever you start, there will be information for you to receive, review, and reflect upon. There is no one system that is better, nor is there an order in which you should explore. Initially, you may feel your mind is directing you, trying to get it right. This is okay! What do you feel, sense, or know? Follow the guidance system of your inner world.

# PART 1

# YOU, CHANGE, AND ENERGY

*The Journey of a thousand miles begins with a single step.*

—Lao-tzu

Are you looking for something new? Do you feel that there is more to life? Is the way you have been living no longer working for you?

Suzan was in this situation at the start of the millennium. Her desire for change and deeper understanding about life and her purpose began an exploration of the world of energy and healing. Looking back, it felt like she was being gently directed by something deep within her toward new possibilities, new ways of living and functioning in the world, yet she didn't know where she was headed or what she was looking for. It seemed to take forever, and, at times, she also felt that she had an impossible task.

She dived into the depths of her being, explored the world of energy and healing from many perspectives, learned and changed so much for the better. Now, two decades later, her deepest desire is to help you find the quickest and easiest way to live authentically, to your full potential, and to share the things she wishes she had known earlier.

Donna was led into the world of energy and healing by curiosity and boredom. She amassed a wealth of knowledge and research and avidly followed new innovations. To this day, she continues to be interested in the new and innovative energies that are coming into our awareness. Her desire is to share this knowledge with you in an easily accessible way.

In our experience, you are not alone—many are feeling a need for change, a deeper understanding and/or sense of purpose. Behind the desire for change is usually a catalyst. You may have experienced a gentle or not-so-gentle nudge—what was previously comfortable is no longer so. Perhaps you have had challenges, health issues, unforeseen changes, which in turn create space for something new to manifest.

**If you always do what you've always done,
You will always get what you've always got**.

—Henry Ford

Many are experiencing unexpected change and turmoil. Previous ways of living are no longer working. We believe this is a wake-up call creating the desire and opportunity to find new, more fulfilling ways of being.

Change, in our opinion, is more accessible now than at any other time in recent history. As mentioned earlier, it is easier, quicker, and requires less effort that ever before. Within the realm of energy lies great potentials and possibilities for positive and lasting change for humanity.

At some point, for many, the challenge of staying in a situation becomes greater than the fear of the new or unknown. All you need is a willingness to change and to accept where you are now. Acceptance does not imply that you enjoy, want, or are proud of a situation—whether past or present inside or outside of your control. It enables you to direct your focus and energy in a new, more positive way. This will allow you to see things differently and begin to move forward.

**(Acceptance does not apply in a situation where your safety and security are at risk.)**

Resistance is common. We have all developed coping strategies and behaviors related to events that we were not able to understand. The time or situation may not have been right; we may have been pre-verbal or not have had the tools or emotional intelligence to understand. Events and circumstances were subconsciously ignored, hidden, buried, or locked away, resulting in a block or interruption to the normal healthy flow of energy, causing dis-ease and discomfort at some level.

New energy has become available in the past few years. You now have the chance to embrace this new energy, quickly and easily removing any blockages and obstacles hidden in your conscious and/or unconscious mind. This is the beginning of the healing journey. It creates opportunities to be happier, healthier, and more fulfilled. Please understand that there is no right or wrong way, only the way that works for you. Just as your fingerprint is unique, so too will be your experiences.

# UNDERSTANDING HOW ENERGY WORKS

The invisible world is made of energy. Everything, seen and unseen, is energy and has an impact on each of us. All thoughts, feelings, and emotions are linked to an energetic vibration. The body vibrates at a frequency that reflets your current state. This is known as **resonance**.

When feeling unhappy or unwell, your vibration will be at a lower rate than if you are happy or in love. Trauma, negative events and emotions have a lower frequency and vibration. These denser energies can cause dis-ease. By freeing the energy and restoring flow, your body can become at ease. This is the realm of energy healing.

Have you ever noticed that when you are with an unhappy person, or someone with many worries and anxieties, you start to feel the same. Even though you were feeling absolutely fine earlier, you now feel heavy, grumpy, sluggish, or negative.

Similarly, if you are with very happy people, you feel much lighter and more positive. Even the thoughts of being with them may increase your vibration. This is the Law of Attraction at work—like attracts like.

Dutch physicist and scientist Christian Huygens first noticed this in the late 1600s, when he observed that clocks near each other began to chime together. If he disrupted their rhythms, they would always re-sychronize. When women are living in close proximity, it is common for their monthly cycles to match. This matching of energies is called **entrainment**. It is the force whereby energy starts to synchronize with a nearby energy field.

There is a whole world of invisible energy with which we continually, albeit unconsciously, interact.

Do you recall a place where you felt very peaceful and calm, and others where you just wanted to leave? Geographic locations hold energy and an imprint of activities that have taken place during history. There is a very different feel in Stonehenge (England) and Gettysburg battlefield (Pennsylvania).

Buildings also have a frequency, and the energies will vary according to the direction they face, their proximity to water, the people who have lived or worked there, etc.

Public figures, people in the street, your family, your colleagues—everyone and everything in your life has an energetic impact.

Your energies are continuously interacting with the energies of people and places, which have positive or negative effects. Knowledge of this energy gives possibilities for its conscious use. It is one way to create positive, life-enhancing change.

# PART 2

# AN INVISIBLE WORLD

...there is some invisible force that is moving every aspect of reality to its next best expression.

—Marianne Williamson

If you want to find the secrets of the universe, think in terms of energy, frequency, and vibration.

—Nikola Tesla

***What if...*** there is a world as yet unknown, of unlimited potential, free from the restrictions of the past? A world of possibility, potential, and power, where you can access answers, knowing, and understanding, a place where positive and lasting changes can be made. It is an innate part of you, perhaps forgotten or overlooked, yet it is still there.

We invite you to become curious, to reacquaint yourself with the connections and resources you have to tap into this powerful world of invisible energy. Put any skepticism aside for now; join us as we explore this world of energy and healing.

This invisible world is made up of many kinds of energy, all vibrating at different rates and invisible to the eye. These are apparent by their effects. You become aware of some of this energy through your senses. You feel the heat of the sun, see trees swaying in the wind, smell perfume, and hear music. Radio, TV, Wi-Fi, movies, electricity, and batteries are part of everyday life. All use light and sound waves, or frequencies, which cannot be seen.

In our earliest history, we only believed what we could see. At times, the sun, moon, and stars were worshipped. Eclipses caused great fear. The telescope increased our world of vision; some stars were revealed as planets. We learned of planets rotating around the sun. Later, more sophisticated telescopes showed galaxies, planets within these galaxies, and what scientists called dark matter. Scientists also discovered that the earth is surrounded by the energies of gravity, electromagnetics, strong nuclear and weak nuclear energy. Now there is talk of a fifth field of energy, for which we yet have no name.

Very little was known at that time about how the inside of the body worked. Now X-rays, MRIs, and CAT scans minimize the need for exploratory operations. Miniature cameras and robotics reduce the negative impact of surgery. Throughout history, there have been reports of energy surrounding people. This energy is called an aura, and it can be photographed with a specialized camera. The image shows colors surrounding the physical body.

This energy that has been known for thousands of years, and is used for healing in the Indian and Chinese traditions. In the Indian yoga tradition, it is called prana, which flows within and around the body. In China, it is known as qi, or chi, and moves through channels called meridians. Although still unseen, these energies are becoming more widely known through the popularity of yoga and acupuncture. Scientific knowledge is now validating what many have seen or believed through history.

Knowledge, understanding, and interaction with the invisible world once were part of everyday life for all people. History saw a disconnection and loss of much knowledge, especially in the West. References became limited to the realm of religion, some of which spoke of invisible angels and/or other spirits who guide and protect.

Patterns of behavior start to develop in the womb. Our personal understanding and beliefs depend on family, upbringing, ancestry, education, and the society in which we live. We learn to act in a certain way as a result of this conditioning. We also learn about health, money, relationships, jobs, and fears in the same way. None of these influences can be seen, but they are an invisible part of our personality and psychology. Many times, we don't even realize that we have these patterns or that they are affecting us.

At this time in history, energies are shifting. Eclipses, astrology and/or planetary alignments are intensifying the energies. New energies are becoming available. Scientific knowledge is rapidly increasing our understanding of what was once invisible, yet there are still undiscovered parts of the universe that we use but cannot see.

R. Buckminster Fuller stated, "Ninety-nine percent of who you are is invisible and untouchable." Psychologists believe that between 80 and 90 percent of the mind is subconscious. Now more than at any other time in history, it is possible to tap into this world. It is free, and the tools needed are within each of us.

An example of the invisible world is seen in the work of Dr. Masaru Emoto. His experiments on water studied the effect of the spoken or written word and music. When positive words, such as *peace*, *love*, *happiness*, and *gratitude*, were spoken to or written on a container of water, beautiful crystals formed. Similarly, attractive crystals developed with music like Amazing Grace and Beethoven's Pastoral Symphony. When negative words—"you make me sick," "anger", "evil"—or heavy metal music were used, the result was a less attractive, poorly formed crystal.

We are comprised of more than 50 percent water. As a simple experiment, surround yourself with positive words and music; notice the effect. This is the power you have to influence your life with the invisible world.

In the 1960s, Cleve Backster was planning some experiments on awareness and response in plants using the polygraph, (lie detector). As he was setting up and preparing, he started thinking about his plan to burn one of the plant's leaves. To his surprise, the polygraph reacted, showing a very high reading to the thought alone. It was as if the plant had heard the thought. Subsequent research found that the plant had a similar reaction when he was in the room next door, further down the hallway, several buildings and/or even hundreds of miles away. It appeared the plant would react to the thoughts of the person it was attuned to, irrespective of distance.

The invisible world is a world of energy, potential, healing, and transformation. It is free, always there, and waiting for you to understand more about it. We would like to share with you a four-step process to access this invisible world. We wish you well in your journey. Hae fun and be open to new possibilities.

**If you can see the invisible, you can achieve the impossible.**

—Shiv Khera

**Your most precious, valued possessions and your greatest powers are invisible and intangible.**

—W. Clement Stone

# THE FOUR I'S

We are permanently connected with the world of the invisible, the subconscious, and the unknown. The doorway is always open. The four I's represent one way to relearn and reconnect. The process appears here in stages, but with practice and/or a remembering, it can become unconscious and automatic:

1. **Instinct** (need) assures survival by triggering an automatic response, which is unlearned and the same throughout a species. It involves a basic need: food, water, shelter, care, safety, and survival.

2. **Intention** (want) is a statement of desire for something to be other than it is. It can be in relation to many things, including work, family, home, life, the arts, or sports performance.

3. **Intuition** (how) is an instant glimpse or guidance as to how to fulfill your desire. It is a flash of understanding, a knowing, or a small, quiet voice.

4. **Imagination** (process) is daydreaming, visualizing, or making up a *what-if* story.

**Need, Want, How, Process**–all work together for the best possible result when we choose to change our life. The four I's will bring us whatever our thoughts (intentions) choose.

Instinct is a need for survival, shelter, safety, food, and water. Any time these needs are threatened or are not met, they become the driving force of life and remain so until fulfilled.

When the core needs are met, your intention is free to explore other areas of life you would like to change. Be sure your intent is specific and clear. State it, then release it to the universe. Give space to intuition. Be open to new ways of knowing and insight beyond your conscious mind. Then, let go of the outcome, stay focused on the intent, and remain positive and present. Allow imagination free reign to explore different scenarios.

Trust the universe. It will align the energies to grant your desire in the easiest way possible for your best and highest interests. Let go of expectations as to how and when it will happen.

Here are the steps of this process:

- Focus on the intent
- Remain positive and present
- Create space for intuition and imagination
- Let go of the outcome (the how or when)
- Trust the universe

Below is a diagram of our understanding of the process:

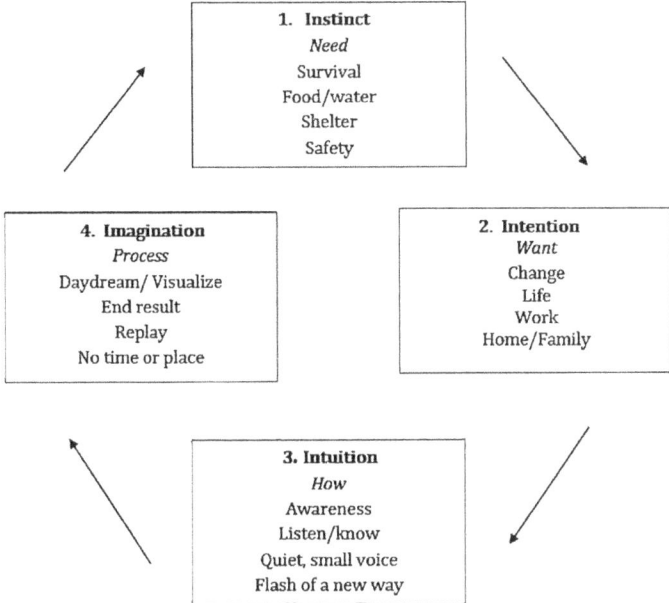

All four I's work together seamlessly; each one builds upon the other—instinct, intention, intuition, imagination. This is the foundation for interacting with our invisible world and is key to understanding, refining, and creating a more fulfilling life. The four I's become trusted friends who assist us in daily life and on our healing journey

# INSTINCT

Need
Care
Food/Water
Shelter
Safety/ Survival

**Even if they don't know it, everyone has the instinct to survive.**

—Rhonda Rousey

**Instinct is a marvelous thing. It can neither be explained nor ignored.**

—Agatha Christie

**Instin**ct (need) assures survival by triggering an automatic response, which is unlearned and the same throughout a species. It involves a basic need, such as food, water, shelter, care, safety, and survival.

Instinct alerts, guides, and helps detect unseen, unheard, and unknown potential threats, to ensure survival of self and, possibly, the group. These threats were a part of everyday life for the earliest inhabitants of earth. For thousands of years, survival was a huge part of everyday life.

Food and water were not readily available; some plants and berries were poisonous. Only those with the most highly tuned instincts had the potential to survive and pass on their knowledge. Future generations' actions and reactions formed from this ancestral learning. As the human world became safer, survival issues were no longer an ever-present threat. Safety and security became the predominant reality.

As humans, we are all born with the same instincts, predominantly the instinct to survive. Instinct is beyond the five senses. It is seen in the movement of the head and open mouth of a newborn searching for food. The abilities to suckle, grasp, cry, and make swimming motions are automatic and unlearned.

Instinct is hereditary and independent of experience. It is our earliest encounter with the invisible world. In humans, the first time an action is performed, it is an instinct; at a very early age, we begin observing and copying others. We learn skills and solve problems through play, conditioning, reward and punishment, communicating by words, tone of voice, facial expression, and gesture.

Could it be that we also have an instinct to explore in order to gain deeper understanding of our world, our origins, space, and more? This possible instinct activates at the appropriate time, usually when our needs are fulfilled and we have created stability and security. Often, it comes in the latter part of life.

All traditions have instinctively looked to a power greater than themselves to gain understanding and meaning. Call it Energy, Source, Oneness, or God.

Instinct ensures survival and is the foundation for later intention, intuition, and imagination.

**Trust your instinct to the end, though you can render no reason.**

**—Ralph Waldo Emerson**

# INTENTION

Want
Change
Life
Work
Home/Family

**Intention is the starting point of every dream, creative power that fulfills all of our needs for money, relationships, spiritual awakening, love; everything that happens in the universe begins with intention.**

—Deepak Chopra, MD

**Intention is not something you do, but rather a force that exists in the universe as an invisible field of energy....**

—Dr. Wayne Dyer

**Intention** (want) is a statement of desire for something to be other than it is. It can be related to work, family, home, life, the arts, or sports performance.

Your deepest desires are brought into being by intention, energized by your thoughts. Each day you have between fifty thousand and seventy thousand thoughts, mostly unconscious. Each thought, whether conscious or unconscious sends energy vibrations into the Universe. The Law of Attraction states that "like attracts like." Negative thoughts attract negative energy and situations. Focusing on positive, conscious thoughts attracts positive energy and situation into your life. Have you ever noticed how confident people who expect success are usually successful. You may think of them as just lucky or having an enchanted life.

Your fears and doubts are the only limitation when setting an intention. What do you really want? Can you believe it is possible?

Express intention as a clear and positive statement of an outcome you want to experience. It must be personal, specific, and in the present tense, as if you are living with it now. ("I am..."). Do not limit or suggest how the process will unfold.

Language is extremely important when setting intentions. Check for words that have negative or restrictive implications, for example:

- *Try* (potential failure or never get)
- *Want* (lack)
- *Hope* (possible defeat)
- *Should* (victim)
- Avoid *always, not, or never*

Consider using words that ensure the process is effortless, peaceful, natural, joyful, harmonious, graceful, easy, et. Some examples of positive intentions are:

- I am joyful in all I do.
- I step into the unknown with grace and ease.
- My body is strong and healthy.
- I am loved and loving.

Start with something small, quiet your mind, and reflect on what you really want to happen. It can focus on long-range or short-range goals, in any area of your life. Write your intention. Review and revise until it feels complete, then release it to the Universe. Let go of the outcome, and be positive that it will happen in its own (not your) perfect time.

Ensure the energy of your thoughts, words, and actions match those of your intention. Watch for doubt and negativity, which come from the ego part of you that is fearful of change and wants to keep things as they are. Treat this part of you as a small child: be kind, reassuring, loving, compassionate, and grateful. Explain that you will keep it safe and that you are using your intention only for the highest and best good of all parts of you.

You may experience events and actions that seem to be the opposite of your intention. Are you complaining, judging, or doubting? Watch for feelings that you may have done it wrong or might be a failure. Treat yourself compassionately and use these opportunities to review and refine your intention. What does it show you? Is it highlighting a behavior or an area of your life that needs to be reviewed? Do you feel worthy of your intention? Are you sabotaging it in some way? You may have to "fake it," and that's okay. Stay positive, and be willing to change your thoughts and actions.

Check in with your intention again, and focus on your desired outcome. This will start energy moving. It is not about being right or perfect. Be positive and open to signs or guidance in all areas of your life and wait for doors to open. Say *yes* to new ideas that come to your attention. Welcome everything as a signal that the universe is helping with your intention. Remember, there is no time restriction: it will take as long as it takes. Appreciate the scenery and opportunities to learn and grow. You will get where you are going at the perfect time for you.

In a nutshell:

- **Be specific** and concise.
- **Be willing** to take the necessary steps.
- **Be determined** to change.
- **Be grateful** for what you have.
- **Release expectation** as to how and when it will happen
- **Allow** the Universe to manage the details.

Now that you have your intention, it's time to bring in your intuition.

**Before you agree to do anything that might add even the smallest amount of stress to your life, ask yourself: What is my truest intention? Give yourself time to let a yes resound within you. When it's right, I guarantee that your entire body will feel it.**

—Oprah Winfrey

Our intention creates our reality.

—Dr. Wayne Dyer

# INTUITION

How
Awareness
Listen/Know
Quiet, Small Voice
Flash of a New way

**... personal intuition—always whispers; it never shouts.**

**—Steven Spielberg**

**Built into you is an internal guidance system that shows you the way home. All you need to do is heed the voice.**

**—Neale Donald Walsh**

**Intuition** (how) is an instant glimpse or guidance as to how to fulfill your desire. It is a flash of understanding, a small, quiet voice, or a knowing.

Have you ever made an instant decision but not known how or why? Perhaps you experienced a flash of insight, a great action plan became obvious, or something just came to you. This is your intuition, sometimes referred to as the sixth sense. It is the inspirational impulse used by artists, business professionals, and creative thinkers, with no thought as to the origin of the "idea".

Intuition is closely linked to, but different from instinct. Whereas intuition is unique to an individual, instinct is the same for a species. You may know it as a hunch, a gut feeling, gut knowing, or a gut instinct. It can be anything from a subtle hint to great leaps in logic. Interestingly, Boston University, Rice University, and George Mason University have reported research that shows intuition is more efficient than logical thinking when it comes to making decisions. Albert Einstein believed that a scientific truth was revealed through intuition, prior to scientific verification.

The conscious mind represents the visible part of a iceberg (10%). Beneath the surface of your awareness is the remaining 90%, your invisible subconscious mind. This is the realm of your Intuition. It is an instant, emotionless, and nonlinear insight, without any past knowledge, proof, evidence, or conscious thinking. You may see, hear, sense, feel, or know, quick and quiet flashes in the form of pictures, symbols, or small fragments of information. No way is right or better: all are equally valid.

Intuition is a powerful tool for guidance. You have always had intuition, although you may not be aware of, or acknowledge, it. The connection may not be strong as a result of lack of use or ignoring its messages. It may be something you have always done, so automatic that you do not recognize it.

The best way to access intuition is by creating space, listening to those inner flashes, and, most importantly, trusting them. Intuitive insight often occurs during meditation, being in nature, just before going to sleep, on waking, in the shower, or even when driving. It is a knowing, without knowing how you know. Messages are spontaneous, fast, automatic, effortless, associative, and beyond control.

If you are unsure whether it is intuition or mind, notice your thoughts. Are they slower, sequential, deliberately controlled, inflexible, or judgmental? If so, it is your reasoning and conditioned mind rather than your intuition.

You can develop your relationship and confidence in your intuition with practice. Pay attention to experiences, give yourself creative freedom in all areas of your life, have fun, and stay positive. All these may enhance your intuitive ability. Meditation and classes can help. You may consider consulting a pendulum, tarot cards, oracle cards, or books at the beginning. However, these are not essential.

Intuition is beyond intellect and may not make sense to your conscious mind. Remember not to judge. Be open to listening to others in a new way; pay special attention to your own inner voice.

Using your intuition is a matter of trusting the voice, however crazy it might seem, and believing that the idea did not come from your mind. Trust that the universe is giving you information you need right now.

Pay attention to, be aware of, and be willing to receive, any information offered. Acknowledge any associated feelings. Intuition does not usually announce itself with a drumroll, but, rather, presents as quiet and subtle messages. You may be guided to attend a workshop, listen to a webinar, take an alternative route, or go to a different store. Just feel, and do not judge: it may bring a solution or be relevant at a later date. Trust that it is perfect for you and for your highest and best good.

Steps for developing your intuition include:

- **Be aware** of your intuition.
- **Listen** to that inner knowing that has no fear.
- **Interpret** the information.
- **Be willing** to do things differently.
- **Follow** that guidance.

**The intuitive mind is a sacred gift and the rational mind is a faithful servant. We have created a society that honors the servant and has forgotten the gift.**

—Albert Einstein

**…don't let the noise of other's opinions drown your own inner voice… Everything else is secondary.**

—Steve Jobs

# IMAGINATION

Process
Daydream/Visualize
End Result
Replay an Incident
No Time or Place

**Those who can imagine anything, can create the impossible.**

—Alan Turing

**Everything you can imagine is real.**

—Pablo Picasso

**Imagination** (process) is using daydreaming, visualizing, or making up a *what-if* story.

Imagination has the potential to change your world and create your future. It is a place of infinite possibilities, where your intention and intuitive knowing may come together in a virtual reality. Information will then have an opportunity to show up in a different manner. Problems may be solved, or new solutions may appear. You are able to try out different actions and outcomes in your imagination and view them as if they are happening now.

When our ancestors began to think beyond their present moment, the ability to see or know things not in their world at that time became possible. This started the process of change, with creative planning, problem solving, and innovating. It was the advent of imagination and creativity in all its aspects.

Imagination, also called daydreaming, is something that we all have. It allows an exploration of more than one idea at a time as *what-if* scenarios, which may start at the beginning, in the middle, or at the end, and are limited only by you. It operates via images, symbols, or objects in the real world. Time is irrelevant; things can be fantastical, inventive, and/or original.

It plays a role in many aspects of innovation, motivation, and enhancing life. Your body cannot differentiate between a situation that is real and/or is imagined. It responds in exactly the same way.. The nervous system is activated, and hormones are released, whether watching a movie or involved in a real event.

Artists imagine a painting before it comes to life. Musicians hear the music in their head before composing a song. Fiction writers and storytellers also "hear" before they write. Poets use imagination to put words together to convey an image. Inventors see the solution before they invent the product.

To enhance your imagination, consider reading widely, investigating new paths of knowledge, being curious, engaging in interesting new activities, expanding interests, developing talents, and exploring new perspectives.

Imagination changes the world around you. It is a creative way to help you achieve success. You are always emitting energy into the universe, whether you are thinking, visualizing, pretending, or simply *being*. Whatever energy you are focusing on, either positive or negative, the universe brings more of it (Law of Attraction).

When you are sure of the desired outcome (intention), spend time focusing as if it has happened and is your new reality. This sets into motion forces that are far more powerful and productive than willpower alone.

Imagination encompasses the invisible world of instinct, intention, and intuition. All four steps (the four I's) flow effortlessly from one to the other, each building upon the previous one to produce a successful outcome. They become trusted friends who assist in our daily life and on our healing journey.

Imagination can be accessed by the following steps:

- **Desire** to change.
- **Write** an intention.
- **Focus** on the intention.
- **Allow** time and space for intuition.
- **Daydream** or visualize.
- **Trust** the outcome.

The universe is benevolent; it will match your energy. Everything is as it should be for your further growth and understanding. Trust, and follow your heart.

**You see things; and you say "why?" But I dream things that never were, and I say "why not?"**

—**George Bernard Shaw**

**Imagination is a gift given to us... each one of us use it differently.**

—**Brian Jacques**

# NAVIGATING THE INNER WORLD OF YOU

The physical body relates to the outer world through sight, hearing, smell, touch, and taste. Similar senses are available to navigate the invisible world; these are known as the "Clairs." *Clair* means *clear* and refers to getting a clear message not otherwise available using physical senses. These are the predominant **Clairs**:

- Clairvoyance is seeing with the "mind's eye", an inner visual.
- Clairaudience is an inner hearing of information.
- Claircognizance is an inner knowing beyond doubt.
- Clairsentience is an inner feeling bringing forth insight and knowledge.
- Clairtangency (Psychometry) is gaining information from the invisible world by touching an object or a person.
- Clairscent is an inner sense of smell that triggers understanding or conveys meaning.

These are inherent in everyone, although one is usually predominant. It can take time to accept and fully utilize these gifts. With practice and trust, they can guide you through life, providing unseen and otherwise unknown wisdom.

There are other gifts as well, although less well known.

**Channeling** allows information from the invisible world to come through you. It is an effortless flow of information and guidance for yourself or another, and it may be expressed verbally or in writing.

Everyone has the ability to channel. Although probably unaware of this most people channel regularly: saying the right words to someone in need or expressing a heartfelt message that flows from pen to paper.

**Mediumship** is a form of channeling that connects with and brings through messages from a deceased relative or friend.

# PART 3

# ABOUT HEALING

Although healing may be unfamiliar, it is not really new to you. Do you remember the loving touch of your mother's hands when you were sick? Perhaps you were given healing herbs, received a blessing or prayer. These are just a few of the healing methods handed down from past generations.

Healing is wholeness, a state of acceptance and peace. It is the process of becoming an objective observer of your life, free to be the highest possible version of yourself and to live in harmony at all levels (physical, emotional, mental, and spiritual).

All levels are linked. What is happening in the mind affects the body, physical symptoms are related to emotion(s), and so on. By developing awareness of our dramas and stories, automatic actions, reactions, and responses, we are able to identify and then heal associated emotional wounds, patterns, and behaviors. When there is calmness and no longer a reaction to these triggers, the healing is complete.

We can be drawn into the realm of healing for many reasons—curiosity, desperation, exhaustion, emotional turmoil, knowing it is right for you, desiring to help yourself and/or others, or searching for answers not available from conventional methods.

You are a natural healer; everyone is a natural healer. For thousands of years, healing has been used in daily life. The ability to heal is innate in all. The requirements are awareness and willingness to change. There is nothing for you to do: the energy and body intelligence do the healing.

Healing takes place by changing the energies associated with unhealthy conditions—thoughts, feelings, and emotions into more positive vibrations of love, peace, joy, well-being, etc. Energy will match the highest vibration available. It can change from one state to another, from one frequency to another; but it cannot be destroyed.

There are many methods of healing: hands-on, hands-off, receiving energetic transmissions or attunements, learning a specific technology and increasing self-awareness. Healing can be in one-to-one sessions, in workshops, groups, classes, in person and online. No one method is right for everyone, or right forever. As you grow, your needs change, and other methods may become of interest.

# CAN I HEAL MYSELF? DO I NEED A HEALER?

Self-healing can be very successful; there is much that can be done through awareness and personal development. It empowers and develops confidence. We recommend you become an active participant in your healing, and we give a six-step "Kick-Starting Your Healing" process in part 4.

There may be occasions when support, learning, and guidance are needed. We can be too close to, or unable to see some issues, often very deep core issues. These take a huge amount of awareness and self-love to explore. In these cases, it is beneficial to use the expertise of a healer. Healers are objective, see the bigger picture, highlight unhelpful patterns and/or blocked energies. Their role is to create space and bring through healing energies for your body to use as needed.

It is great to explore and find what works for you. After a time, it may be helpful to have one main modality and/or practitioner with whom you develop a relationship and come to trust. When the healing is maximized, it is time to move on. Sometimes you may linger for longer than needed; that will be fine too. Trust your inner guidance. You will know intuitively what is right for you.

Each modality works at an energy frequency; the practitioner vibrates at a complementary frequency. You will be drawn to the frequency that resonates best for you at that time. If, and/or when, something else is needed, your inner world will guide you. At this time, thank the practitioner, your teacher, and move on.

# YOU ARE YOUR OWN HEALER

**I**t **is important to understand that you are your own healer**. You may not yet know or understand this, but healing is hardwired and innate in all humans. You have the ability to make great change(s) within yourself, the power to block any healing energies you do not want or for which you are not ready.

For those who experience lack of confidence and would like support of like-minded people, we suggest joining a group and/or attending person-growth workshops.

A journal which records your thought and experiences may also be supportive. Many find it very affirming to look back and see progress. New insight and/pr awareness may become apparent.

# PART 4

# KICK-START YOUR HEALING BY CHANGING YOUR THINKING

Here are six simple steps for personal development and healing, which can rapidly improve how you see yourself and your world:

**1. Willingness to Change**

Many experience fear of change as an insurmountable obstacle. It is not necessary to leap off the cliff. One step at a time is sufficient—one step can change your focus and direction. Just be willing to change.

**2. Self-Awareness**

Self-awareness is developing awareness of thoughts, feelings, emotions, and behaviors behind your actions and reactions. It is receiving and noticing input both—external and internal—from body, mind, and senses. The process is ongoing.

**3. Acceptance**

The next step is accepting and owning all parts of you, including those that are hidden, disliked, or ignored.

Acceptance is simple and free; it can be done anytime and anywhere. It is allowing whatever is happening to unfold in its own time, irrespective of whether it is pleasant or unpleasant, convenient or inconvenient. It does not mean that you agree, disagree, want, or reject anything. Rather, you simply observe and let it be okay.

**Remember—acceptance does not apply in a situation where your safety and security are at risk.**

The act of acceptance removes the need for a situation to be other than it is in the present moment. Resisting what is happening or holding on to something that happened in the past is the cause of a huge amount of pain and anxiety. This release allows and facilitates the flow of energy and movement, taking you to another, more comfortable, place.

However challenging or beyond comprehension it may appear, everything happens to help you grow and evolve into the best possible version of yourself.

## 4. Forgiveness

Forgiveness for self and others, whether victim or perpetrator, cuts ties to the past, freeing oppressive energy. The result is new possibilities for and wellbeing. Again, it doesn't imply agreement with or validation of a behavior or event. Many find forgiveness frees them to move forward with life.

## 5. Gratitude

Gratitude focuses on everything in a thankful way. Understanding and accepting that all experience is for our growth makes gratitude much easier. It may be helpful to start with something small: *I am grateful for the air I breathe, food to eat*, etc. The more you practice, the more there is to be grateful for, and the more refined gratitude becomes. Every event has been part of shaping you into the person you are, even the less positive experiences. A deepening appreciation increases your sense of well-being and peace of mind.

There are many ways to practice gratitude—meditation, prayer, ritual, verbal expression, and written expression (gratitude diary or journal). Experiment to find the most effective method for you.

## 6. Love

Love is honoring and appreciating all that you are, your uniqueness, your gifts, and your challenges—past and present. This is the place of real peace. It is only when we accept and truly love all aspects of the self (warts and all) that we can see clearly, and truly love another. The more we focus on self-love, the higher our vibration becomes, and we start to radiate this energy of love. It ripples out into home, family, workplace, etc., drawing to us more of the same (Law of Attraction).

**Please note**: It is not possible to change others; however, by changing ourselves, the world around us changes. It will be for your best interest, which may not be apparent immediately, but become so with hindsight.

**Self-love is the key to transforming your personal world and the world at large.**

# PART 5

# TWENTY-FIRST-CENTURY HEALING MODALITIES: ARTICLES CONTRIBUTED BY GUEST AUTHORS

This includes a selection of lesser-known healing and self-knowledge modalities that were developed for the twenty-first century. We feel that they all offer something valuable. However, as previously mentioned, there is no right technique, and none are better than others. It is simply a matter of what is right for you at any given time. Explore more twenty-first-century healing modalities in part 6.

We are grateful to our guest authors for submitting articles on each of their particular modalities and feel it gives a real flavor of their respective approaches.

# AUMAKHUA-KI® ENERGY BALANCING & MEDITATION

### Rev. Ojela Frank

AumaKhua-Ki® (om-ah-koo-ah-kee), increases a person's capacity to channel more healing energy and elevates their consciousness to higher states of awareness. Most workshops and webinars include a powerful AumaKhua-Ki® Attunement, complete instruction in AKEBM therapeutic techniques, experiential, energetic exercises, session work, a manual or handouts and an AKEBM Class Certificate. This unique and proprietary information is passed from a certified AumaKhua-Ki® Instructor to the student.

## What Makes AumaKhua-Ki® *Truly Unique*

Message from Rev. Ojela Frank, founder of AumaKhua-Ki@ Energy Balancing & Meditation:

I have been on the path of seeking and searching since 1969. I explored many paths wanting to discover how to know BLISS. Twenty-three years after doing energy attunements, I channeled AumaKhua-Ki® in 2009 while doing three months of kundalini meditations. Over the next three years, I channeled more AumaKhua-Ki® symbols for Awakening. January 2013 is the official year that AKEBM began as a new energy system for modern times. It continues to evolve and take form.

As of August 2017, there are now 18 AumaKhua-Ki® symbols and 19 mantras. (Each symbol has an activating mantra.) After I became a Reiki 1 & 2 practitioner in 1983, I took an interest in spiritual initiations, attunements & energy activations. In 1984, I also studied with a woman Ethel, who inpiree me tot know that there fould ge other energy systems that had symbols and attunements that worked similar to Reiki. (Ethel Lombardi was formerly a Reiki Master trained by Reiki Gran Master Mrs. Takata).

Later, I became a Reiki Master in 1989 and did Reiki Attunements on initiates. But, it was the crystal healing attunements that I did in 1986 that propelled me into the path as an Initiator. The attunement work became upgraded as Spirit led me to doing energy activations, group activations and remote activations over the years.

I experienced a second spiritual rebirth in 2009. I journeyed inward activating my chakras, raising my Kundalini, becoming a qigong instructor and doing a summer of advanced energy meditations. When I realized the sacred gift that was given to me, I came out of retirement, went to massage school became a licensed massage therapist and continued my journey as spiritual teacher. By end pf January 2013, I decided to share what I was experiencing...hotter hands, upper chakras activations and energy waves pulsating through my body when using the AK Energy. I developed AumaKhua-Ki® Energy Balancing & Meditation as a multiple level course program. At the onset, it included 10 AK energy symbols and an Atlantean healing mantra. In the beginning, there was only myself, hot hands and living at a higher frequency. Could this be passed to others?? I already saw reactions in the energy sessions with clients (for 3.5 years). But could I initiate others into the AumaKhua-Ki® Energy? The answer became YES!!! Now, there are other AumaKhua-Ki® Instructors who are also doing the energetic awakening attunements.

Throughout most of my life, I studied several energy systems that used symbols. AK Energy Balancing & Meditation is very high frequency, especially at the advanced AK Instructor levels. Knowing this, AK is stronger than anything I've studied in 48 years! What certified AK Instructors share in AumaKhua-Ki® classes, and pass through the AK Attunements to initiates, gives shortcuts to experiencing and knowing Awakening—that took me more than four decades to acquire. Students can learn the equivalence of this in less than one year with AumaKhua-Khui®.

If you want an opportunity to grow, experience a spiritual revolution beyond the mundane to nourish your spiritual life, AumaKhua-Ki® IS a Path of Awakening. I never dreamed that I could experience this in my life, but I have! And, I look forward to sharing this sacred energy wisdom with others who are open and ready to KNOW their Soul Consciousness and have deeper communion with the Divine.

Ojela and the certified AKEBM Instructors have made it their life's work to help people achieve higher states of spiritual evolution through total energetic activation and initiation with AumaKhua-Ki®. Living in the energy and frequency of AumaKhua-Ki® enhances your health, intuition, purpose, ability to serve and consciously design your life; which in turn, enhances your well-being in all areas of your life.

## Aumakhua or Khua means Higher Self
## Ki means Universal Life Energy

AumaKhua-Ki® IS a potent path to activation and connection to your highest self. AK Energy Balancing Levels 1 through AK Energy Master Class include an AumaKhua-Ki® Energy Attunement. Some of the advanced AK Instructor classes include higher frequency attunements.

AumaKhua-Ki® Energy Balancing & Meditation offers beginner, intermediate and advanced workshops and webinars. There are several certifications available:

AumaKhua-Ki® Energy Balancing 1

AumaKhua-Ki® Practitioner 2, 3, 4

AumaKhua-Ki® ENERGY MASTER

AumaKhua-Ki® TEACHER 1, 2, & 3

AumaKhua-Ki® ENERGY MASTER Practitioner

AumaKhua-Ki® MASTER INSTRUCTOR 1$^{ST}$, 2$^{ND}$, 3$^{RD}$, & 4$^{TH}$ degree

AumaKhua-Ki® Grand Master 1st & 2$^{ND}$ degree

**Type**: hands on, symbols, distant & remote, self-practice, sessions, high frequency energy meditations altrered states (advanced levels).
**Learning Method**: in-person or online, AumaKhua-Ki® Energy Attunements needed (in person or done remotely), workshops, webinars and retreats.
**Website**: https://www.facebook.com/akenergytraining/

# BREATHWORK©

## David Elliott

There are many forms of meditation, and many emphasize attention on the breath. In the two-stage Pranayama breathing meditation that I teach, there is a very specific focus on using the breath as a tool to:

1. Quiet the mind;
2. Relax the body;
3. Bring attention to the energy in the body;
4. Activate an energy flow through the chakras and nervous system
5. Learn to direct the energy flow to places where energy and emotion are stuck in the body;
6. Clear the stuck energies;
7. Quiet the mind to an even deeper level (i.e. the Delta state);
8. Bring the breather to a spiritually awakened point where there is a profound experience between the breather and their Spirit, and/or a merging of the two.

The two-stage Pranayama breathwork process is done lying down and consists of two deep inhales followed by one deep exhale. (Two stage simply refers to the two-inhales in this practice.) All breathing is done through an open mouth. The first breath is accessed deep in the low belly. The second inhale moves the breath from the low belly into the high chest. Then both breaths are exhaled through the open mouth.

That's it. Two inhales followed by a full exhale—all done through an open mouth. This continues at a steady pace that can be sustained for about twenty to thirty minutes without pushing too aggressively. It's important to clarify that we are not hyperventilating it's more like the kind of breathing you might experience during steady exercise, like fast walking or climbing stairs.

Classical yogic texts describe prana as the energy of the universe and *pranayama* is defined as the regulation of the breath through certain techniques and exercises. Increasing the oxygen in the bloodstream via the two-stage Pranayama breathwork practice activates the hypothalamus gland/crown chakra. As the gland is stimulated, endorphins are release, which trigger other energy centers in the body. The breather starts to feel energy move through the body and nervous system.

This is where the meditation starts to take on its own special expression, and this is why I always say that the Universe is holding the agenda for the healing, not the breathwork practitioner. The breather can feel this; many have very deep personal experiences that I really don't even need to interpret. That's why I feel like the breath is the doorway to the Spirit.

The shortest meditation I have created is seven minutes, and the optimal length is about twenty to thirty minutes. It takes about six to seven minutes for the brain to stop thinking and start to relax. I call this the masculine or active part of the meditation. The first six to seven minutes is where the strongest resistance come up as the brain fights to stay in control.

Everyone's physiology is different, but after about seven minutes of consistent two-stage breathing, the energy starts to shift for most people. This is when we start to move into the feminine or receptive part of the breathwork practice. While there is still active engagement with the breath, the breather finds more of their own rhythm and experiences less resistance. The brain relaxes, the emotions become activated and clear or move, and the heart begins to open as the person feels their energy moving.

Some examples of emotions moving might be a person experiencing sadness and beginning to cry, whereas in their normal day-to-day life they may suppress this sadness or not allow themselves to feel it enough to let it move. If they struggle with anxiety, they may start to feel cold as the breath brings attention to this anxious energy. Similarly, if anger is stuck in the body, there will likely be some physical symptoms showing up as tension. I have observed over decades of teaching with thousands of students that if the breather keeps breathing and allowing the emotion to express itself, it will move.

About two-thirds or three-quarters of the way through a practice depending on what a person or group might need — we shift into the relaxation phase of the meditation. We can transition by inviting the breather to take one inhale and one exhale through the mouth, and then to breathe normally, in and out through the nose. No effort. In this relaxation phase, the breather might have a range of experiences — from ongoing release of emotion, to feeling a bit "high" or ecstatic, to a sense of peace, as their heart expands and they connect to and/or merge with their Spirit.

A breathwork session is a creative experience — I use music and healing tools like sage and essential oils to support the movement of energy. We also can use laughter and yelling to create space for change in the body. Often we find that emotions get stuck in the throat, so we keep the throat chakra open and don't have the breather's head propped up on a pillow. This posture — and laughing, yelling or other vocalization —creates an opportunity for emotions to move through the throat, supporting the opening of the heart. Additional tools include eye masks and ocean stones for the breather to hold in each hand. To keep them grounded to their body and the Earth.

There are so many benefits of breathwork—from clearing stuck energy to transforming negative beliefs and patterns, to connecting someone with their Spirit. From my perspective, one of the most important benefits is that in breathwork, the healing experience is claimed by the one needing the healing. The art form for the healer/breathwork/actioners to not do too much in the process or to take responsibility for the experience. This is what sets breathwork apart from many other healing modalities, therapies and support systems that may be more dependent on the practitioner. Breathwork is a practice you can always do on your own. You can choose to change your condition and your life simply by lying down ad practicing this active meditation.

While breathwork can help people release and heal their bodies very quickly on their own, I should also say that the process can be greatly facilitated by working with a trained practitioner to support the experience. The partitioner can witness and guide the breather through the experience. The practitioner can witness and guide the breather through difficult spots while still leaving the breather in control of the experience; there should be no feeling like the breather needs the healer to replicate this experience to do the work.

This work can be done individually, and also in groups led by a trained practitioner. The group dynamic and energy flow adds a layer of community and deepens awareness of self and others as each person moves through their own healing journey. I have found that people who have a balance of breathing solo and breathing with a group make tremendous progress towards personal healing.

***I am not able to give you the exact mythological roots of this work, but the CliffsNotes are that a healer named Tim Heath showed up in my life in 1989 and told me that I was a clairaudient healer. He told me I had been a healer in many lifetimes and this was another one of them. He also said that I taught him this two-stage Pranayama breathwork meditation some two thousand years ago in India, and that he came to reintroduce me to the work in this lifetime because he needed me to help him again. He informed me that he wasn't my teacher, but rather a guide to help me remember. After Tim led me through my first breathing session, he would ask me to work on him during most visits.

It was all very surreal at the time and caused much reluctance in me to call myself a healer, but close to thirty years later it all makes more sense. I know one day I have to travel to India to see what this land holds for me, but in the meantime I am busy training people to do breathwork in other parts of the world.

I have written a couple of books about the healing work. *The Reluctant Healer* describes the work and chronicles my early journey into the healing process that I use and teach today. My second book, *HEALING*, is a much more in-depth, step-by-step process of how to heal your life. Over the years I have developed my Healer Training courses, Levels 1-4, creating a course structure to develop and support individuals who have the desire to heal themselves and others.

While breathwork is the foundational tool I use in my healing work, there are others, such as: developing intuition; the use of essential oils; and the practices of gratitude and creative expression. They all dovetail into the phrase, "Where Awareness Goes, Energy

Flows." On the deepest level we are teaching people to wake up, to learn to love themselves, to be aware of all that they are creating, and to live life to their fullest potential.

People have repeatedly asked me why I have not trademarked Breathwork or created a 'catchier' name. The work I do is not about the marketing or trying to create any more commerce than what I have experienced over all these years. It's not about what I can charge people or profitability. It's about the exchange.

I agreed to help others and make this work my primary focus back in 2001 because it became apparent that this was something I had to do.

This journey has been amazing and I'm grateful for each and every experience I've had along the way.

**Type**: healing sessions—in-person, hands-on, intuitive, energetic, daily practice with downloadable guided meditations from website https:// davidelliottstore.com/categories/Audio/
**Learning Method**: In person classes—Healer Training classes teaches people how to do the healing breathwork—http://ww.davidelliott.com/training/
**Online classes--workshops**—Global Healing Group EVENT schedule—http://www.daidelliot.com/category/eventlist/
**Website**: http://www.davidelliott.com/
**Books:** Elliot David. *The Reluctant Healer*. Los Angeles, Ca.: Hawk Press, © 2005
Elliott, David. *Healing*. Los Angeles, Ca.: Hawk Press, ©2010

# DIVINE HEALING MASTER KEY

### Dr. Ahlmeirah Ariel Hallaire

## What is Healing?

The concept of healing basically means to come into wholeness, the fullness of who we can be, the full expression of our potential. It is based on the understanding that each and every one of us is, at our core, a being of light, love, truth, peace, wisdom and power. Unfortunately, this beam of light we hold within us is often covered up with layers of programming, limiting beliefs about ourselves and the world, traumas and shock and toxins of different kinds. So, in essence, our light is blocked out to varying degrees. The more our light is blocked out, the more we feel unhappy, blocked, frightened and the more our health suffers.

The purpose of healing is to remove these layers of fear, erroneous beliefs and pain. As the process of healing occurs, more and more of our inner light shines through and our life improves, our health recovers, our relationships become more loving and open, our gifts and qualities naturally find ways of expressing themselves and we feel joy, happiness and at peace. The process of healing is like parting the clouds so that the light of the sun is revealed. It feels natural, like a coming home to our true nature.

## What is Divine Healing Master Key (DHMK)

DMHK is a form of spiritual healing. In all forms of spiritual healing, the healer accesses Spiritual energy, which is of a higher vibration or frequency to the physical, energetic, mental and emotional bodies. This "Higher Frequency" has the power to reorganize what is in chaos, to put back things in their right pace, to release blocks and lower vibrational energies: in other words, it has the power to heal.

## How is Divine Healing Different fo other forms of Spiritual Healing?

There are many forms of Spiritual Healing. Most of them have been channeled through either the angelic realms, the Ascended Masters or the Higher Light Beings that are assisting the Ascension of Planet Earth.

DHMK is different in that it comes from all three realms, namely the angelic, Ascended Masters and Higher Light Beings. The Elohim or Creator Gods are also at the root of this powerful modality. When it was channeled, a co-creative effort was made in the higher dimensions by these different realms to bring through a tool that would help humanity and would be able to appeal to all types of people.

Another aspect of DHMK which makes it stand out is that it is "multidimensional" in nature. This means that when you receive healing with DHMK it works on many levels all at once, such as the present, your past lives, your ancestors, your parallel lives, your future lives, your soul, your body, your emotions, to name but a few. The effect of this is that the healing effect is very powerful and much faster than with many other healing modalities.

## Who is Divine Healing Master Key for?

When DHMK was brought through, it came through a small team of experienced healers who all had the same goal: to create a system of healing that was easy to learn and easy to use. We wanted to empower our students to be able to heal themselves instead of being dependent on having sessions. Many of our clients are people on an accelerated path of growth. When this occurs, many layers of disconnection and pain come up for healing very rapidly and in rapid succession. This rapid process can make you feel very dysfunctional and weighed down. DHMK was designed to be used on an as needed basis by the user who is going through a process of rapid change and growth.

Of course, it is also possible to receive one-to-one sessions of DHMK. These can be done in person or online, as time and space don't exist when we do spiritual forms of healing.

## What happens during a DHMK session?

I have been training therapists in DHMK for over 15 years internationally and so there is a growing body of well-trained therapists. A session will usually start with the therapist asking some questions about what issues need addressing. The chat can last up to 20 minutes and helps to create a rapport between client and therapist.

After this you will be invited to lie down. Indeed, when we are relaxed and comfortable, healing is much easier and deeper.

The therapist will then do a series of opening commands or prayers. These set the energy and create a safe space for the maximum healing to occur. All healing is always dedicated to the highest possible service.

During the body of the session, the therapist will use the manuals to ascertain what needs clearing, balancing or brought to awareness. They will use a combination of muscle testing and intuitive guidance during this process. Command codes are used to clear the layers successively. The processing is gentle, graceful and effortless. As each layer releases, people often feel lighter and lighter, a sense of relief, a sense of rightness and as if they are coming back to themselves progressively.

## What are the benefits of DHMK?

DHMK addresses all issues pertaining to the human journey on Earth. It can clear past life issues. Ancestral issues, childhood issues, current blocks in life such as unconscious sabotages, relationship issues, conflicts and addictions. It clears spiritual and soul issues. It heals the physical, energetic, emotional/mental and spiritual bodies. Physical issues and diseases are addressed too, as their root cause is in the energetic and psycho spiritual.

In general, the longer an issue has been present, the longer it will take to heal. Some issues are cleared in one session only. For example, I worked with a lady who suffered from insomnia for several years. It was a simple case of energetic interference which was easily cleared. She wrote to me afterwards about her delight at sleeping well again, and about how impressed she was that it took just one session.

Other issues may take longer to heal: I worked with a lady who was profoundly depressed. When we started, she had just recovered from a suicide attempt. It took 12 sessions, to get her back on her feet. By the end of those sessions, she was back at work, feeling like life had meaning once more and that she had a valuable contribution to make. Moreover, she had acquired some deep insights into the root cause of her depression and was making some major changes in her life so that she felt more aligned with her truth.

## How can I learn DHMK?

Training in DHMK is a valuable investment in your personal development. At the moment, I Ahlmeirah am the only trainer from the original group of healers who channeled the system. I have trained one other teacher, Nicolas David Ngan.

There are 5 levels of DHMK, each level is at a higher level in frequency to the previous one and has a particular theme. The theme of the Level 1 group is Self-Empowerment, and learning this level alone will allow you to work on yourself and others as they are also practitioner trainings.

The groups are usually 4 days. They can be done in person and on-line. There is a course manual for each training. The training is experiential, which means that you receive a lot of healing, and also learn to give healing during the group.

It is my intention to train more teachers in the forthcoming years, thus allowing the work to spread.

**Website**: centreofloveandenlightenment.net
**Email**: ahlmeirah9@centreofloveandenlightenment.net

# ESOTERIC NUMEROLOGY

### Donna Linn

Numerology uses the numerals 1 through 9 to describe understanding within the birth name and the date of birth. It calculates the numbers for the inner personality, outer personality, destiny, power, life, and missing numbers. Esoteric Numerology is an extension continuation of that numerology. It encompasses hidden knowledge within the tens and hundreds, which most numerologists do not use or understand. Earlier, one number was used for three letters, but I was given knowledge regarding how to use each letter as a specific number.

## How Did I Learn About It?

I was given this information over a summer between school years in order to help me understand the dynamics of children from the blended family resulting from my second marriage. In published numerology books, I saw very little correlating each letter (A to Z) with their corresponding numbers (1 to 26).

One sentence in Kevin Quinn Avery's book (*The Numbers* of *Life*) led me down the path of employing the birth date to find out more about what had happened, was happening, or will happen within my life. As I followed the number sequences, I was amazed at the knowledge staring me in the face—just coming from my birth date. Questioning kicked in: What happens if one section of the date is considered at a time? What if you add the numbers together? What if you subtract the numbers?

Patterns began emerging, sometimes several times within these sections. What does this mean? How can I use this information?

## What I Discovered

*Master numbers* are hiding in plain sight within the higher numbers. Are they useful in this time frame? Is there a new level of growth that we need for the present moment? How does this operate with what is already known? Is it very old knowledge being brought back into this time? While only 11, 22, 33, and sometimes 44 are used in previous numerology, tI believe here are also higher master numbers: 55, 66, 77, 88, 99, 111, 222, etc.

Utilizing subtraction from 10, 100, and 1,000, I observed numbers from the master numbers, which I refer to as *initiation numbers*. I understand these numbers as a way to access the power of the master number.

The *reversed numbers* (e.g., 41 and 14) are the same numerals with different place value. As an elementary-school teacher, this caught my attention. The tens (10s) place is more important than the ones (1s) place, even though they both reduce to one (1).

If you can add something, you can also subtract it. With trial and error, several charts later, I realized that subtracting gives you additional information. Not finding this in any numerology book, I named one the *core of light*, and the other *psychic ability*.

Here are some of the discoveries:

1. There are more master numbers than we know. Master numbers have initiation numbers.
2. Reversed numbers differ only in weight by place value (i.e., 1s, 10s or 100s).
3. Timing is indicated for important events that have happened, will happen, or are now happening.
4. A family profile slows similarities and differences for each person
5. Triangles, diamonds, and parallelograms can be created within the master numbers
6. All years repeat in patterns—or what I call "stems"—and each relates to a specific energy.
7. Patterns for years are based on only three sets of numbers.
8. Millennia coincide as "stacks," one upon the other. The only difference is the twenty numbers at the beginning (1-20) and the end (80-100).
9. There is a way to get additional information from an arbitrary conception chart.

## How Does It Work?

The birth name and the name in use now display hidden numbers. All numerologists use the same terms--inner personality, outer personality, destiny, power, life—and follow the same methodology. The difference is that I use each letter (A to Z) with a specific number (1 to 26).

Using just the date of birth (month, day, year, time), there is information for the physical, mental, emotional, and spiritual areas of life. These "stems of dates" describe specific time for learning lessons, receiving gifts, markers for change, or important events. It *does not* tell you *what* will happen, only *when* it will happen.

Each piece of the birth date introduces three to nine numbers, or what I call "stems of years." Things that have happened are more likely to be apparent if noticing more of the same years. Every choice—made or not made, before now or now—has consequences. None are bad or good. It depends on your attitude toward the specific event. Sometimes all that is needed is to have an awareness of a situation. Esoteric Numerology just gives an indication of the timing of the choice.

## In Closing

You can get a short or long reading with the numbers and insight about your life in person or on Zoom. Or you can learn to do this for yourself, your family, and your friends by reading my book, *Breaking the Code*.

It is now time for me to share this information and reach out to more people who are interested. This can by means of a chart, a workshop, or just talking about the numerology.

I am pleased to present to the world at large my way of finding numbers that have been hidden in the numerology within names and dates of birth—what I call Esoteric Numerology.

**Type**: Short or long individual readings
**Learning Methods**: In person, via Zoom, in two-day workshops
**Email**: 2donnamessick@gmail.com; Subject Line: Numerology
**Books**: Linn, Donna. Breaking the Code
    Linn, Donna. Beyond the Code (Sacred Geometry)

# GALACTIC HEALING®

## Joy Kauf

Welcome to Galactic Healing. From the first time I heard about this modality, I knew this was the one I was destined to teach. When I started performing Galactic Healing session it was like a whole new world opened to me. I ha numerous light beings start working with me to formulate this healing modality. I was certified in other healing modalities: however, they did not touch my heart the way Galactic Healing did. I was fortunate to be able to purchase Galactic Healing from my teacher and once the sale was finalized, it began to change. I had a being I will call the "Blue Lady from the Blue Star" appear to me and she began changing a few symbols and rearranging them in a new order. Once this was done, I began teaching Galactic Healing as the modality it is today. So, let me share with you the modality that was given to me by "Blue Lady from the Blue Star". (Also known as "The Blue Mother").

Before I go into the different levels of this modality, I want to share with you the different way I work with the chakras. You may be accustomed to working with the 7 chakra centers within the body. With Galactic Healing, you work with 10 chakras and at times I have been guided to add an 11$^{th}$ chakra. I start working at the sole of the feet, then the ankle, then I move up to the knees. I then go in the order of the chakras—root, sacral, solar plex, heart, throat, third eye, and crown. Over the past two years, I have been guided to work on a client's umbilical center and add the symbols there as well. If you feel that pull, then by all means, include that center as well. The umbilical center is between the sacral and the solar plex.

So let's get into what Galactic Healing is. Galactic Healing as a modality heals on three levels. These levels are the Shamanic Frequency, the Angelic Frequency, and the Sacred Geometry Frequency.

The first level is the Shamanic Frequency. The Shamanic Frequency heals on the physical plane. This level brings the body into balance with the elements of earth. Generally speaking, a person has some level of imbalance to the elements of air, earth, fire, and water. We have all had past lives where one of these elements have brought about our demise. This frequency, along with the symbols, brings us back into balance with these elements. You also become connected to the earth.

The Shamanic level has two additional symbols that stand for Spirit and Remembrance. These symbols are placed in chakras starting with the soles of the feet. This allows the person to become more fully aligned with earth and with themselves.

The second level is the Angelic Frequency. The Angelic Frequency heals on an emotional level. This level brings the clients into balance with their emotions. A person carries their emotions in their etheric field and this frequency helps to remove the lower vibration emotions before they can be absorbed into the physical body. Each symbol is connected to different Ascended Masters and Archangels. These symbols are placed into the client's energy field. You will clear the Etheric Field first by placing the sacred symbols over the subject. You will then clear each chakra starting with the feet. After that you will place the different sacred symbols into each Chakra with love and intent. Before you finish, there is a sacred symbol that is sprinkled all over the top of the client's energy field. I visualize this symbol as gold and I see it clearing the client's energy field. You then seal these symbols into the etheric field with Protection. Protection is the final symbol used as a sealant within the energy field.

The third level is the Sacred Geometry Frequency—the I AM that I AM. This is a very powerful frequency and is one of my personal favorites. This frequency is able to heal at a soul level. It also full integrates all three frequencies within the client's energy field. Thiis level as eight sacred symbols where the previous levels only had six. On this level, you integrate sacred geometry symbols into the energy field of your client. This level allows for deeper "investigation" or "speculation." When I use these symbols I see them in my mind's eye as three-dimensional holographic symbols, being placed into each chakra. I have had clients open up and become in tune with sacred beings. Some have also reported becoming more connected with spiritual realm, vivid dreams, as well as emotional releases over days following the session.

Galactic Healing is about harnessing the Galactic Energy and bringing the feminine and masculine divine to join with it. Every person has male and female aspects, so this will assist you in integrating these frequencies to create harmony in your life. You will feel greater peace in your mind, body, and spirit.

I would like to share a story about animals and Galactic Healing. I used this healing on my German Shepard who had bad hips. Getting up and down was so hard for her. When I came home, I would rub my hands together and she would literally back up th receive the energy. I had the veterinarian tell me she would need to be put down at 10 years old. She outlived her expectancy by 4 years.

Clients have reported that this modality feels like they are in an altered state and they can feel the energy moving through them. I have had several clients look at me and ask, "if you are working on my head who is holding my feet?"

If you are interested in being certified as a Galactic Healing Practitioner, we offer in person classes. You will receive a training manual, an attunement and a certificate. We also offer online webinar intro workshops as well.

To find out more about Galactic Healing, like us on Facebook at Galactic Healing, call (or see) Joy Kauf at the Miracles of Joy Metaphysical Store, Lewisville, Texas. 972-221-8080; www.miraclesofjoy.com. She is also co-Creator of the Galactic At-One-Ment Healing Modality, and creator of the Miracles of Joy Webinar Series.

**Type**: Energy healing, hands on/off, remote and in person.
**Learning Methods**: Online or in person.
**Website**:
https://www.miraclesofjoy.org/galactic-at-one-ment-workshop.html

# HUMAN DESIGN

**Chetan Parkyn**

As we begin to learn to embrace the Aquarian Age, one thing has to be clear: no one is coming to rescue us. Whether Jesus, Buddha, Mohammed or any other gifted Being or alien ever had that inclination, it's not happening.

We are here, and we are here to sort our life, we are here to live this miracle, to have this experience and to take full responsibility for it, because on some level we made that agreement.

The times of blaming the teacher, the boss, mother, the "man", the "system", or God are over. We are obliged to live our own life as a conscious presence in human form with as much access to Universal Truths as anyone else.

This is it, plain and simple.

Yes, there is great assistance from sources unseen, however, the responsibility remains ours. Having high hopes and positive thinking is one possibility, accepting reality with clear creative intention is another.

When we comprehend this, we become aware of all the opinions and beliefs we've absorbed from perhaps well-meaning sources, and the things we've taken for granted that in no way assist us in our lives, at least towards being fulfilled.

It is reckoned that 70% of working people are disengaged from the work they do; that much of their day is spent watching a clock until it is time to access a paycheck and go looking for 'freedom' outside of the workplace.

If more time is spent relating to a computer, television or mobile device than in actually relating with people or the world around us.... is it a wonder that the planet on which we live and the nature around us are in trouble

And there are still wars, guns, bombs and armies, even after NASA and The Russian Space Agency took photos of our home, Mother Earth in the early 1960's.

There has to be a shift on consciousness. We have to grow our awareness and appreciation for what we have been given. We must move beyond the fear of death and learn instead to embrace and celebrate life, for that is our reality while we are here.

And fortunately, we've been given an amazing device to help us do that. Human Design was given to us in 1987. It is a 21st Century self-remembering device. It gives us a clear blueprint for our life. It illustrates exactly what we came here for and how to live that out to the best of our ability and with the greatest fulfillment.

I remember quite clearly being told about Human Design in 1979 during a reading in India, with a "Shadow Reader," (Chhayashastri), a full eight years before Human Design actually came into being.

I had just turned 28, a qualified and practicing mechanical engineer, and I was in India involved in learning meditation with the enlightened mystic, Osho. The "Shadow Reader" was working with another system and from materials written several millennia previously, and who in a 25-minute session completely changed the understanding I had of my life's trajectory, forever.

You might have had experiences in your life when the hairs go up on the back of your neck because you know you are being touched by something that echoes deeply in your being. This reading was so profound because it described so many things about me that resonated...and without my knowing quite how.

Among other things, I was told to "get ready" for a new system that would be coming into my life, because I would be "doing the same work" as the man who was reading for me, "helping people wake up to who they really are.

He told me about the books I'd write, the readings I'd give and the hundreds of thousands of people all over the world whose lives would change as a result. From that day onwards, on the advice of the Shadow Reader, I started reading for people...hands, cards, faces, tea leaves auras, astrology, I Ching, etc.,..." to be ready," as he suggested, for when this "new system" would come into my life.

Sure enough in 1993, I received a chart, my Human Design chart sent to me by an old friend. I recognized the chart immediately for what it was, and my own journey with Human Design started.

Human Design is a gift to humanity. It is a transformational device... it is a means to trigger conscious transformation into each individual's life. It is the first objective system in that it clearly illustrates the design of your physical, mental, emotional and ultimately spiritual environment as a unique individual for every moment of your entire lifetime.

Human Design is objective in that it illustrates your very own blueprint. See how this blueprint has a particular signature and way of working for you, and all of a sudden you are in present tense, in the 21st Century, as a conscious, creative presence, ready for whatever life presents to you.

One particular aspect of Human Design is unique, in that it gives us direct access to inherited (unconscious) characteristics that are passed on to us from our ancestry. Even realizing that this information exists and being able to give it a clear description clarifies so many puzzles in our lives.

We are here discovering, expanding and creating in this life experience. And as we move deeper into the Aquarian Age, we watch as our lives shift into new forms and patterns.

Over the years and through the many thousands of Readings and Trainings in Human Design I have been honored to give, I have been met with tears, shrieks of delight, deep silence and blissful wonder when relaying what I've seen in someone's Human Design.

Existence does not duplicate anything, and so knowing and honoring your unique individuality is essential… and Human Design illustrates your individuality perfectly.

People have told me that they feel recognized, perhaps for the first time ever. They feel settled, reassured and suddenly realigned in their lives. They see not only their own life in a whole new light, but also instantly comprehend the ways of the world around them.

When you live attuned to your own nature, you no longer have to take on "borrowed" concepts, ideas, traditions and formalities that distort your reality. When you are at home in your own life, you are no longer subject to worries, concerns, fears, and ultimately disease that have nothing to do with you.

Human Design is in its very early days of development, and more study and research will be needed before it becomes instrumental in rearranging many of the world's systems, like communications, education, business, health and other realms. Imagine schools, for example, where children are provided education according to their way of learning.

When people know who they are and live according to their own nature, and then they expand that knowing into their work, schooling, health, diet and the lives of other people around them, suddenly the world takes on a whole new dimension.

I ask you to have a deep look into your Human Design and to appreciate that you are here, with remarkable potential, in this miraculous experience we are calling life. Contact@HumanDesign ForUsAll.com to find out about Readings, Trainings, Reports, Books and Downloads. www.HumanDesignForUsAll.com for Free and Comprehensive Reports giving a full description of each individual's life.

www.TheHumanDesignApp.com for iOS and Android Human Design Apps...The Free App draws up Human Design charts and describes several aspects of the chart. A fee-based expanded version of the App calculates Combined Relationship Charts, Transits and provides more extensive details about Human Design.  Producer of the Comprehensive Human Design App for iphones, Androids, Tablets, and more: http://thehumandesignapp.com/

**Type**: Readings, Counseling
**Learning Methods**: Online or in person
**Email**: www.HumanDesignForUsAll.com (1) 760 298 0918
**Books**:
Human Design Discover the Person You Were Born to Be

The Book of Lines, A 12st Century View of the IChing the Chinese Book of Changes

Co-Author: the Book of Destinies, Discover the Life You Were Born To

# MIR-METHOD®

### SELF HEALING TO BE USED AT HOME!
### Be the MIRror of the change you want to see in the world!
### Mireille Mettes

The MIR-Method was created in the Netherlands. It was a series of coincidences, cooperation with patients, intuition and hard and intensive studies that led to this method. You can use it on yourself, without needing to buy anything. It was developed in 2009 by Mireille Mettes. She gave the MIR-Method free to the world, as a gift. The name "MIR" stands for "Mental and Intuitive Reset". "MIR" also means "Peace" in Russian. She wishes everyone peace in their minds, hearts and lives. That's why she set the MIR-Method free. "Heal yourself, heal the world!"

## How does it work?

The MIR-Method consists of two parts: one is to make your active brain relax. Only then you have access to your subconscious. You do this by gently stroking your hand.

The other part is to give active commands to your subconscious. These commands tell your subconscious to heal yourself. Every phrase (called 'step') is pronounced 3 times.

So in total you stroke your hand, and keep stroking while pronouncing these 9 phrases 3 time. Have a look at the video to see how it works. It is really easy!

**The 9 steps of the MIR-Method**

1. Optimize acidity.
2. Detox all toxicity.
3. Detach father. Detach Mother
4. Clear meridians.
5. Supplement all shortages.
6. Balance hormone system.
7. Fulfill basic needs.
8. Optimize chakras and aura.
9. Clarify mission.

# Why these words?

Mireille used muscle resting to find the exact words needed for self-healing. The subconscious needs direct commands, however they need to be quite broad, so the body can figure out what to do. Often, we think we understand the body, and science has discovered so much. But we do not understand the total mysteries of the body, yet. And it is best to leave the healing processes up to the body! It knows what to do and how to do it!

# Why does it work?

Touching your own skin has several purposes. It makes you feel relaxed and open to suggestions. It makes your active brain feel safe, so it steps away for a moment. This is a good thing, because most problems are caused by out brain that can often be over-dramatic.

Touching your skin also gives you a sense of contact with yourself. It brings you back into the here and now and strengthens your focus.

The words are commands for your subconscious. If the commands are precise enough the subconscious can activate your body to heal itself. It does this by letting go of old emotions, by detoxing all kinds of matter that is in your body and that shouldn't be there. It adds your energy, so your 'batteries' are recharged again. And it helps you with the alignment for your purpose here on earth. Mireille states that: "People who are astray from their life's path, fall ill." So it is very healing to remember your talents, your longings, the things you like to do best, because that brings you back to your life's path. "Doing what you came here for, is pure bliss!"

## For whom is the MIR-Method® intended?

The MIR-Method is for people with **emotional and physical problems** who would like to do something about it themselves. The MIR-Method re-activates your body's self-healing ability. It is easy to do and can be done in your own home. It can be used with anyone. If you have a disease, start carefully with only step 5 and 7 for two weeks. After that, continue with all 9 steps.

## Doing the MIR-Method®

You can find everything you need to know on the website: www.mirmethod.com. It only takes 2 minutes twice per day. Watch the instruction video at the website for more explanation. In addition, you need the perseverance to continue the method for at least 4 weeks. For support, register on the MIR-Method website for six weeks free support tip e-mails. You will also receive chapters 1 — 3 of the M IR-Method Handbook for free.

## We enjoy helping you

A team of MIR-Method coaches is ready to help you use the MIR-Method. They are trained to help the MIR-Method work more profoundly with respect to your specific needs. Coaches can help you, for example, if you have a strong physical reaction, through a difficult period, or because it seems to be taking too long.

## Don't believe in it, just do it

*Mireille: "It's not necessary to believe in it. The laws of nature involved in the MIR-Method work for everyone. It differs from one person to another how much you notice its effects. You can only really evaluate that the MIR-Method has done for you after 4 months."* You can use the MIR-Method on children and animals.

## Think realistically

The MIR-Method is never a replacement for medical or psychiatric help. Use your common sense and keep in touch with your doctor or specialist. Continue to use your medication(s) faithfully for as long as your doctor or specialist thinks it is necessary.

## About Mireille

Mireille Mettes is a naturopath who closed her practice once the MIR-Method was complete. Prior to this, she taught English and was an Educationalist. Because of her background in education, teaching people is her greatest pleasure. This is what moved her to make her MIR-Method available to everyone. The more people work with it, and the more autonomous they become, the happier she becomes!

At the moment, Mireille spends her time spreading the MIR-Method. This means giving lectures, answering emails and people's comments, and writing about new information that is interesting for people who want to use the MIR-Method. Mireille says, *"My hope for you is that the MIR-Method does you a lot of good!"*

## Mireille's support team

The greatest support to Mireille's work is her husband, Remco. He created the website and takes care of all administrative work. Together, they cooperate to further spread the MIR-Method worldwide, supported by a number of volunteers with large hearts!

**Type**: Self-healing, hands-on, online training
**Email**: office@mirmethode.nl
**Website**: www.mirmethod.com
**Book**: MIR-Method® Handbook available from www.mirmethod.com

# THE ESSENCE OF LIFE

### Julieanne Conard

The Essence of Life is a Source energy—an energy that flows from Spirit to animate life in the physical form. Because it is a Quantum energy, instantaneous healing or re-balancing can occur on all levels simply basking in this energetic. Alcazar, the guide of The Stargate Experience, began to teach Julieanne how to re-access and cultivate the energy in 2013. Two years later, once she mastered to creation of near instantaneous abundant flow of The Essence of Life, Alcazar asked Julieanne to teach a group of women how to access and cultivate The Essene of Life within their own energy fields, and how to use this energy for deep relaxation, self-healing, and self-love.

The Essence of Life energy is a facet of Source energy that constantly is available as it flows through from your Beingness into the physical. When you learn how to cultivate it, you can create a very strong Essence energy field—anytime you wish. The Essence energy feel soothing, beautiful, energizing, and naturally "youths" or rejuvenates, your body as it vibrates your energy field.

The Essence of Life has the inherent property of dissolving imbalances effortlessly as it moves through your body. It contains within its flow the perfect blueprint of physical, sensory, mental and emotional vitality. As one basks in this energy, an emergent, tangible sense of one's true Self or Beingness, effortlessly begins to arise. This energy brings you back to your true state: effortless, flowing, and free. Many people experience a feeling of bliss while immersed in the Essence of Life.

The Essence moves like nectar, and holds you on a physical, mental, and emotional level so sweetly that you begin to release whatever is being held, and the holding pattern. This happens gently and effortlessly as you are coaxed into deeply letting go of whatever is not the "real you".

And so in this way the Essence energy work offers a "reset" with Source energy - resetting you to your natural state, which is a blissful relaxation, an energized flow of life force energy.

On a mental level the Essence energy can help to dissolve disruptive thought patterns that repeat, causing cycles of misery. It's as if the Essence surrounds the mental thought patterns, helping them dissolve like the dispersing of a cloud. What's left is a sense of spaciousness and the freedom to choose the thoughts one wishes to embrace.

On an emotional level the Essence can also surround hard, stubborn or difficult feelings with its gentle embrace. Emotions are then soothed, acknowledged and honored while being held at that higher vibration. This allows them to be easily seen, understood, and dissolved - they no longer control you.

On a physical level the Essence seems to move like water, dissipating and eroding aches and pains as it percolates deeper and deeper into the tissues, bones and organs. Again, Essence energy surrounds the imbalance, gently loving it back into a more perfect balance.

The Essence energy is one that must be experienced in order to be understood. As a Quantum energetic, it flows with an intelligence of its own, but also responds as you use your intention to direct it toward certain body areas or mental or emotional patterns.

Once you discover how to connect to the Essence, you never lose the ability. Every time you work with the Essence your connection gets stronger and happens more swiftly, and becomes more effortless. Many report reaching a level of mastery where the moment it's invited the Essence of Life instantly and brightly flows through the whole body and energy field. This sometimes happens quite spontaneously—and it's a total delight. The Essence of Life is also a portal to "home"—to awakening—to the beyond. Because of this, it also accelerates the re-accessing and re-remembering of your own innate spiritual gifts and abilities.

## Julieanne's Personal Journey Toward The Essence of Life

The Essence of Life was first brought to my awareness by a beautiful female channel of Kryon, who began a late December 2012 session as such:

*"Greetings Dear One I am Kryon of Magnetic Service,*

*The energy speaks to one who recognizes what choice is, what quality of life is, what abundance of life force in all its shapes, color, and sounds is all about....*

*There is an attribute within you that has yet to evolve and expand itself...And this attribute we are going to call The Essence of Life."*

The whole session was about The Essence of Life, and I was captivated by the power of Kryon's words and the energies that they hinted at.

Still, it came as a surprise when, three months later, in the process of working with Alcazar to heal traumatic impacts from my childhood, The Essence of Life found me.

To explain this, it's important first to understand this: The Essence of Life is a Source energy, and one way that this Source energy flows through our physical bodies is as sexual energy.

What Alcazar helped me to realize was that due to a huge and sudden shock, as well as rejection and fear that I felt from my parents and deep personal shame - I had disconnected from my own sexual energy when I was a very small child.

Alcazar explained that this sexual energy is one of the most misunderstood energies within humanity. It's often denigrated as dirty or sinful, when in fact it is inherently beautiful and healing - a vital part of our life force energy. Alcazar helped me to understand that one cannot shut down one's own sexual energy without also closing the door to The Essence of Life.

A major aspect of my healing came from honoring and appreciating my own sexual energy - and inviting it to flow again. And, interestingly, when I did this, I found that the quality of appreciation and love kicked the sexual energy into its higher octave. The Essence of Life then began to flow into my body and energy field, demonstrating its natural ability to dissolve imbalances on all levels. Alcazar guided me in this process: to focus on The Essence of Life - to invite it to flow up my torso, into my arms, down the legs - and slowly slowly throughout my whole body.

As the Essence flowed areas of pain or tension would come into my awareness, and Alcazar would guide me to connect with my innate intelligence - the smart body - to sense the deeper cellular memory that was being held.

Usually a memory would arise: a moment when I couldn't cope with what was happening or didn't allow myself to vocalize my truth to someone. Sometimes I would simply get a sense of "I need love" from my body, and Alcazar would guide me to send love - simply with intention.

Once Alcazar helped me to remember a past life as a priest—an experience of being stabbed in the back while attempting to prevent a church from being robbed. The key to recalling that past life memory, was as simple as tuning into a particularly knotted area of my back and alcazar asking me, "What does it FEEL like happened there?" My response, "It feels like I was stabbed in the back…" Spirit has a way of helping us to remember what we already know!

After the underlying truth, story, or feeling was found and expressed, the physical pain could be released. Alcazar guided me to surround the area with the Essence of Life energy. It felt as if the Essence teased apart the condensed sensation of pain until, slowly slowly, the pain dissolved completely. What was left? The Essence of Life in all its sparkling radiance and perfect balance.

**Type**: Channeled Information, Live Energy Transmission, Self-healing, Energetically Encoded Audios, Self-practice
**Learning Methods**: in person and Online Workshops, Personal Session
**Website**: The StargateExoperience.com/essence

# THE SPIRITUAL NUMEROLOGY OF MOSES "READING YOUR SOUL INTEGRATION MAPS"

Joseph ZatKeell Syverson
aka *Yosefahniel Tarkcah*

**Are You Ready to Decode The Greatest Mysteries of Your Life?**

*"Everyone Has A Purpose In Life... a unique gift or special talent to give to others. And when we blend our unique gifts in service to others, we experience the ecstasy and exultation of our own spirit, which is the ultimate goal of all goals!"*
*\*Deepak Chopra MD*

What if "THE ANSWERS" to "THE BIGGEST

QUESTIONS" of your life, were truly all accessible right now... would you have the courage to enter the secret code to unveil them all?

Who Am I? Why am I here? How do I transcend my life's repeating challenges, once and for all? Where can I focus my energy and time to find the greatest fulfillment and happiness?

Why do I have such a difficult time creating _____ in my life? What is my ultimate life purpose?

Believe it or not... the answers to all of these questions and more, have been secretly hidden in your names and birthdate, by the Soul, that you are.

"In the beginning was the Word, and the Word was God." Sound is creation. The sound of your name(s) carries with it the specific vibrations of the Soul. When decoding these vibrations through the Spiritual Numerology of Moses, you literally see the set of experiences at a physical and spiritual level that the Soul has set out to experience in this lifetime.

My wife Mary and I have run a Transformational Coaching Business for 24+ years. The biggest challenge in personal & spiritual growth, is the subconscious beliefs and programs that keep people stuck (ex: It's not safe to show my true self.). 95% of these dysfunctional behaviors/beliefs are unconscious programs from multi-generational trauma, and then we have childhood trauma, imprinting and toxic parenting on top of that. The ego is designed to hide all this from our understanding (so we can survive), so people spend years in therapy, coaching, and filling themselves with medication and often don't change very much at all. You can't transcend or change, what you can't see. This System is very different from other types of numerology. First, this system has the ability to not only de-mystify, but profoundly explain every situation you have found yourself in, or will find yourself in. It is based on the Tree of Life, from Kabbalistic Teachings. Kabbalah (meaning to receive) refers to how the Upper Worlds, or higher dimensions influence our reality in every That is where this system of numerology and our Soul Integration Map Readings, have been a game-changer. Illuminating clearly the unconscious patterns and a treatment protocol would in the past, take us weeks and months... AND now we speak to and reveal this, in the the first 90 minute reading session. When someone sincerely wants to grow and the truth is clearly delivered in a loving & undeniable way, magical transformation JUST happens!

This system is based on the creative energies of the moment of our life experience.

This System, also incorporates The Tarot, I-Ching and Astrology, which covers the full range of possible experiences for a Soul Incarnating onto the earth. There is a set of 22 channeled symbols, which correspond to the 22 Hebrew letters, that actually transmit an energy and connection to the Soul.

We have created 22 medallions that incorporate all the above correspondence, letters, numbers and symbols along with powerful videos and manuals to make it easy for spiritual seekers to learn, contemplate, and even channel messages directly from the Soul, using this system.

The greatest joy in our professional life has been providing **'Soul Integration Map'** channeled readings and healings, to our clients, loved ones, and especially to mothers.

When clients hear and feel how the Soul designed the life they have lived, they often cry and experience a great release of some kind. It's as if the Divine Truth being shared and channeled through the reading, is a beautiful beam of light shining down that instantly dissolves misperceptions they have held about themselves, others and God.

If you are a parent, a spiritual seeker or practicing some form of coaching, counseling, alternative therapy/healing work, this system will upgrade your journey, wisdom and value immensely! If you are a mother and you want to know how to best parent and guide your family... then you just found a hidden treasure chest of jewels.

The gift of learning this work, allows you to guide others to fully embrace and overcome their life's challenges by understanding the jewels hidden inside them, and focusing on their gifts and specific resources, that have the most power to create transformation.

Over the last 13 years, we have utilized this system to raise our children, who are now in their early twenties and thriving, heal our marriage, overcome financial loss and health issues, and we have worked with hundreds of families to support them in understanding family dynamics and how to see their life, with the eyes of their Soul.

The Spiritual Numerology of Moses, has only been available since 1980 and was channeled by the Soul of Moses, Dr. Frank Alper. However, the origins of this work date back thousands of years, when the Tree of Life and Star of David were first introduced. Dr. Alper's mission with this work, was to lead people to developing their intuition up to the full integrity of personality and Soul.

We have expanded on the original system a great deal and have developed 11 levels of training, we call *Soul Psychology Training*, and it's taught over an entire weekend virtually and in person. We also have online classes, where we meet one time per week for 4-8 weeks as well.

**The Mystic Rising Academy** co-founded by Mary & Joseph present: Soul Psychology Training (SPT) based on The Spiritual Numerology of Moses

## SPT1: Soul Psychology Training
"Reading Your Soul Integration Maps"

**SPT2: Soul Integration Maps - Your Mission**
"Dive Deep Into Your Greatest Life Purpose"

**SPT3: Soul Integration Maps - Your Family**
"Develop compassionate understanding of those you love"

**SPT5: Soul Purpose Relating - Hidden Factors**
Illuminating The Sacred Contracts In Your Key Relationships"

**SPT4: Soul Mission Activation**
"Channel Specific Mission Objectives"

**SPT6: Soul Revival -** "Divine Remembrance"
"Past Lives, Pre-Life Planning Room, Ancestral Healing"

**SPT7: Soul Mission Templates** "Mediumship & The Akash"
"Unlocking Your Divine Purpose Mission"

**SPT8: Soul Integration Coaching** "Your 5th Dimensional Team"
"Empower others to Actualize their Soul Mission"

**SPT9: Soul ReIntegration Healing**
"Becoming a Vessel for Divine Alchemy"

**SPT10: Soul Business Coaching**
"Enlightenment Entrepreneurship & Mediumship"

**SPT11: Soul Mission Galactic**
"Galactic Heritage, Meta-Abilities & Your Starseed Missions"

At some point on the Quest, we have to stop worshipping God outside, and embrace the awesome power of God inside... so we have the courage to complete the Soul mission we designed before our birth!

If you would like to receive a reading, attend a free webinar, or speak to us about upcoming trainings or private mentoring, please visit our website or email us:

**Website**: www.TheMysticRisingAcademy.com
**Email**: YosefTarkcah122@gmail.com
**Phone**: 828.774.9837
**Type**: Reading, channeling, counseling, healing
**Learning Method:** Workshop, online, in person, zoom

# THE STARGATE EXPERIENCE

**ENERGY MEDITATIONS TO ACCESS YOUR SUPERCOSCIOUSNESS
EXPERIENCE THE STARATE—
A DOORWAY TO OTHER DIMENSIONS**

**Prageet Harris**

The Stargate Experience will introduce you to a totally new way of evolving your consciousness. No need for hard work, just relaxing and allowing your Superconsciousness to elevate your human experience.

The Stargate is an interdimensional doorway—a geometric structure that emits a powerful conscious energy, an energy that can move participants into a deep meditative space within moments.

The Stargate is a gift from the Beyond, given to Prageet by his guide, Alcazar, in1989. The intention is to support humanity in its awakening by connecting individuals in a tangible way to the numerous benevolent guides that are available to assist in this planetary evolution.

Prageet and his partner Julieanne have shared the Stargate with tens of thousands of people in many countries around the world, and have created The Stargate Experience Academy to share these experiences online.

Each experience with the Stargate is unique, including both meditations and wisdom from Alcazar channeled through both Prageet and Julieanne. With the group intention, the Stargate accelerates its vibrational rate and starts to emanate frequencies from higher dimensions. This supports those present in raising their own vibration effortlessly. In this higher frequency they are far more sensitive to other dimensional beings, their guides who bring their presence into the room to greet and acknowledge those present.

The multi-dimensional energies that radiate from the Stargate and the guides touch each person at a very deep level, often creating change in their lives. Many people have reported experiencing:

- Healing and balance of their physical body
- Clarity of understanding and major insights into their lives
- Deep relaxation with stress dissolving
- Personal karma and unresolved issues being released
- Latent healing abilities being activated
- Recalling past life experiences, wisdom, and skills
- Spontaneous activation of inner vision and psychic abilities
- Growing awareness that they are not just this human aspect - they are their Superconsciousness experiencing through the body
- Greater flow and synchronicity manifesting in their lives

Another amazing aspect of the Stargate work is that it operates in the quantum field. What does this mean? The physical Stargate is an anchor for a higher dimensional consciousness, which we call the "Etheric Stargate." This consciousness is outside of the physical reality in the quantum field where there is no "time."

So individuals can call an Etheric Stargate to come to them and support them in their meditations, raising their vibration to a higher level at any moment, anywhere. This means that Stargate energy meditations that we guide "live" can be experienced anywhere in the world simultaneously, in fact even meditating to the recorded meditations can be felt just as strongly because the energy comes from the quantum field the moment you are meditating.

In this way thousands of people around the world have meditated with us, all feeling the loving energies of the guides at the same moment a massive energetic of change entering the human morphic field!

To facilitate greater potential for people around the world, Alcazar has asked us to produce smaller, "personal" Stargates that can be purchased as amplifiers for personal meditation. They also act as receivers for the global Stargate energetics from the Stargate Energy Grid, the energetics that connects every Stargate around the world.

Our guide, alcazar, describing the Stargate work:

"The Stargate Experience is not about healing. It is about **rebalancing**. It is about bringing you back to the vastness that you are. The Stargate is a leading-edge deice brought to humanity to assist in your awakening and your enlightenment.

How does this differ from so many other techniques that are offered? Firstly, this is not about relieving old pain and suffering, far from it. It is a gathering in groups of like-minded people, and relaxing into a high-dimensional energetic field into which enlightened beings are invited. Both Enlightened Masters from your Earth, and those whom we call Star Families from around the universe, benevolent beings ready to assist in humanity's evolution. As you relax with these beautiful beings, who create around you, and within you, an extremely high vibrational field, your beingness starts to respond.

Your beingness yearns to vibrate I those frequencies of enlightenment, of pure balance, pure openness and, if you are willing to let go, to release the limiting patterns that you have lived for this and many other lives.

*If you are willing to relax and allow self to evolve, then your beingness is free to realign itself So, change then happens. It happens because you can allow your vibration to elevate. You can allow those fears that have held you back to dissolve in the beautiful energetic of oneness.*

So what happens? Change happens on many levels. Change can happen on the physical level, the level of the body. Many people throughout the years of the Stargate work have found their physical body changing within moments, or within hours, or within days. People have reported cancer disappearing; a blind lady getting her sight back; a deaf person getting her hearing back. All kind of physical ailments disappearing, why? Because they have allowed the cause, the emotional or mental issue behind the dis-ease, to simply dissolve they let it go. Sometimes this let go has to occur consciously, many times this let go can occur without any thought about what it is that has been holding you back.

All the Stargate experiences are guided by ourselves, this one Alcazar. We have introduced many techniques to support you in the understanding and letting go. It is the nature of your current mind for most of you, that you think you need to understand before you can let go. Therefore, these techniques have been introduced.

One that we will mention, is that which we call the Stargate Inner Child Work. Very different from techniques that have been used in the past with the inner child. For we operate at the level of the quantum field where you, the adult, can talk to, reassure, and love your inner child; your inner children in fact. And as you love them, as they feel secure, honored, recognized, the limitations that they have created for your adult self-dissolve. Almost immediately, your life becomes that much easier, more joyful, more abundant.

Another technique that we have introduced is that which we call Youthing, where we bring energies to you which actually work on the level of your cells, your DNA, your mitochondria, your stem cells, and so on. Participants become aware of their bodies responding, functioning better, youthing happening!

*So techniques are shared within the overall energetic of the Stargate energy fields. These enable you to relax and let go. With the let go, your energy, your awareness naturally rises. No effort is required. The only effort is the effort that you put into holding back your evolution, your evolution, your holding on to these old patterns.*

*Beloved ones, allow the Stargate experience to gently coax you, persuade you, support you in letting go of all your limitations. So you can naturally rise. Your vibration, your consciousness can naturally rise to connect more and more fully to that which we call your Superconsciousness, your Quantum Self. The Stargate experience is not a healing technique. The Stargate experience is a pathway, a rapid acceleration towards your own enlightenment. It is there for a few courageous ones who are drawn to it."*—Alcazar

You will leave The Stargate Experience more relaxed, uplifted, and amazed. You have just felt the presence of benevolent beings—Angels, Ascended Masters, and some of the benevolent civilizations from around our Universe. Your DNA is now vibrating at a higher level, **and you can feel it.**

**Type**: Channeled Information, Live Energy Transmission, Energetically Encoded Audios, Self-Practice

**Learning Methods**: In person ad Oline Workshhops, Personal Sessions, Facilitator Trainings

**Website**: TheStargateExperience.com,

# PART 6

# TWENTY-FIRST-CENTURY HEALING MODALITIES: A SELECTION OF INNOVATIVE NEW TECHNIQUES

## Anusha Healing

Anusha is a star energy that vibrates at an extremely high frequency, bathing recipients in pure love and light, enabling them to end the frenetic search for something outside themselves and come home to their inherent knowledge and wisdom.

It features twenty-eight symbols, addressing a range of issues from alleviating physical pain, anxiety, and depression, to grounding, balancing, and protecting: from releasing ego-based patterns and behaviors, to anchoring a person into fifth-dimensional living characterized by peace, love, joy, and forgiveness.

Anusha is delivered via hands-on healing by drawing or blowing the symbols into the person's body, chakras, or aura. The experience is deeply relaxing, comforting, and uplifting.

# Biologic Decoding® and Biodecoding®

Biologic Decoding® and Biodecoding® require the client to have a diagnosis of an illness from a medical professional. Both view current illness as a symptom of a past event.

Through discussion, the therapist explores various ages and event in the client's history, building up a picture and unraveling the story until it gets to a trigger event. Clearing this brings about resolution, enabling the energy to flow freely and the body to regain health and well-being.

Biological Decoding incorporates psychogenealogy. Biodecoding includes the principles of NLP (Neuro0Linguistic Programming). Both integrate the concepts of German New Medicine.

# Celebration of Being

At a Celebration of Being, Rites of Passage workshop, you are led through a series of activities to process wounding around the masculine and feminine, to heal the heart, and to create happy, healthy relationships with self and others.

A sacred circle creates a powerful holding energy. It is a safe, secure, confidential, non-judgmental, and loving space. Here, you may venture into the hidden aspects of the self, and from this place magical transformation can happen.

It is a holistic process using the body, mind, and emotions, with personal and group processes, culminating in an individual Rite of Passage. Many experience deep healing, acceptance, freedom to live and relate authentically from the heart.

Celebration of Being is known as COR in the Unites States.

## Chios® Energy Healing

Chios® is an aura and chakra healing system. It uses energy, color, and light to help the client clear the root energetic issue of afflictions and limitations, common conditions, and serious illnesses.

Chios® has sixty-two techniques for healing. Levels 1-3 can be learned from the book, *Chios® Energy Healing—Powerful New Techniques for Healing the Human Energy Field*. By Stephen H. Barrett, and free online resources. Attunements are available from Certified Chios® Master Teachers, although these are not essential.

## Eden Energy Medicine

Eden Energy Medicine was created by Donna Eden who clairvoyantly observed blockages in the flow of energy and experimented with techniques to clear them. This method brings together aspects of acupuncture, kinesiology, yoga, and tai chi to restore energy, health, and well-being.

Techniques are simple and can be done easily and quickly at home. They include tapping or massaging specific energy points (acupoints), tracing energy pathways, meridian lines, exercises, and postures. Her "daily energy routine" takes between five and seven minutes and helps maintain a healthy energy flow and immune system.

Eden's book, **Energy Medicine for Women**, includes practices for hormones, menstruation, fertility, pregnancy, birth, and menopause.

Sessions, workshops, and specialized advice are available from certified practitioners.

# Emotional Freedom Technique® (EFT)

EFT frees blocked energy behind negative emotions by tapping on a series of points around the head, torso, and hands. It is a simple, relatively quick process that can be done at home or with a qualified practitioner. There are reports of benefits with a large number of emotional conditions, including post-traumatic stress disorder (PTSD).

The subconscious is reprogramed by tapping on various points in a specified order, while simultaneously speaking aloud the words "even though I... (negative statement or story). I completely accept myself".

EFT was developed in the 1990s by Gary Craig and has similarities to acupressure, which originates in Traditional Chinese Medicine (TCM).

# Energy in Motion® (EMO)

EMO combines attention, intention, and energy to transform the blocked energy of negative feelings and emotions to restore the natural flow of energy. The process starts by identifying the site of a feeling or an emotion, then setting an intention to release the feeling or an emotion, then setting an intention to release the blockage. Relax while maintaining the intention and focus until the energy flow is felt.

The feeling or emotion is then revisited, and changes are noted. If needed, the process is repeated to clear at a deeper level.

Anyone who can feel can learn EMO at a two-day in-person workshop or an online course. Additional training is available for those who want to become practitioners.

## Men's Groups

There is no longer a recognition of the transition from boyhood to manhood. Roles and ways of life are changing behaviors that were acceptable are no longer so. An increasing number of young men grow up with absent or part-time role models and do not learn the emotional skills needed for a harmonious life. It is no longer clear what it is to be a man.

Men's groups, with their elders and rites-of-passage ceremonies, offer a path of support and guidance to embrace the healthy masculine and take it into everyday life. Some offer regular groups and mentoring.

Groups usually include a form of spirituality and may be faith-based; some have specific targeted audiences such as adolescents, offenders, etc. Examples include the ManKind Project (MKP), the Band of Brothers, Illuman, the Male Journey, MensCraft, and others.

## Metatronic Healing®

Metatronic Healing® uses the very high vibrational energies of Archangel Metatron and his team to "lift the story" and activate the heart connection with the true self, beyond any personal story.

At each level of training, practitioners receive energy transmissions, which are brought in during healing sessions. These energies may include any of the following: metals, crystalline, cosmic, ascended beings, and energy rays.

The lifting-the-story process first identifies an issue or pattern. The client will lie down or sit and relax; further energies are then brought through Metatron to bring deeper awareness to the issue.

The process of lifting the energetic charge of the story begins, and healing can then take place.

Sessions may be in person, remote, or in groups. Metatronic Healing® was developed in 2007 by Pippa Merivale.

## Quantum Touch®

Quantum Touch® combines specific breathwork, the body's natural intelligence, the healing power of touch, and energy to clear the underlying cause of dis-ease.

It is a very simple technique that anyone can learn, including children. Muscle testing and specific techniques focus on and amplify life-force energy, significantly raising the frequency of the healer. This energy transmits through the healer's hands to the client's body, which attunes to the higher frequency, facilitating the self-healing process.

Quantum Touch is a hands-on technique, although a hands-off alternative is available if required.

## Reconnective Healing®/The Reconnection®

Reconnective Healing® balances the body's energy and reconnects the client to the energies of the universe. What makes it unique is that it is hot a technique; nor does it require symptoms or a belief that it will work! It is a very simple process backed by in-depts scientific research and validation of the energetic process.

If you're lucky, your healing will come in the form you anticipated; if you're really lucky, your healing will one in a form you haven't even thought of, one that the universe has in mind specifically for you. –Dr. Eric Pearl, founder the Reconnective Healing®.

## The Body Code®

The Body Code® communicates with the subconscious mind by muscle testing, to find and release trapped energies.

The Body Code® was developed by Dr. Bradley Nelson, a chiropractic doctor and creator of The Emotion Code®. It balances nutrition and lifestyle, energies, circuits and systems, pathogens, toxins, and misalignments, as well as emotions. This restores good health, abundance and happy relationships.

Sessions are available with certified practitioners.

## The Emotion Code®

The Emotion Code® believes that trapped emotions are the underlying cause behind 90 percent of pain. A blocked emotion is identified using a chart and muscle testing (kinesiology). There is no need to connect with, discuss, or relive the emotion.

The blockage is released using a magnet. Emotions are cleared one at a time. The process is repeated, if needed, until optimal energy flow and equilibrium are restored.

*The Emotion Code®* is available as a free book or audio download, from which you can learn the system for self-practice. Certification training is available, as are sessions with certified practitioners.

## ThetaHealing™

ThetaHealing clears limiting beliefs, replacing them with positive alternatives, to bring about physical and emotional well-being. Although based on meditation and prayer, it is suitable for all religions and aims to develop closeness to the Creator. Following the principle of ask and you shall receive, it requires total trust in the love of the *Creator of All That Is* (whatever this means to you.)

Sessions start with a discussion of the issue. The practitioner enters a deep, meditative theta brainwave state and uses a yes/no process and muscle testing to find and replace a limiting belief.

The process continues as the practitioner digs to find the core limiting belief. The practitioner will then command the Creator remove this belief and replace it with a positive one. Energy is then able to flow freely restoring health and well-being.

## Women's Circles

There are a growing number of groups where women of all ages come together in community and sisterhood to share, listen, advise, and support each other. It is a time to honor the feminine: her cycles, her stories, and her wisdom. Often there is little or no hierarchy or structure, and the sessions are guided by flowing intuitive feminine energies.

If you are interested, look for Red Tent Women's Circles, Sacred Women's Circles, Women's Sharing Circles, or Women's Temple. See what is available locally.

# PART 7

# ESTABLISHED HEALING MODALITIES: PRE-TWENTY-FIRST-CENTURY HEALING

## Acupressure

Acupressure clears and balances the flow of energy, or chi, within the body to stimulate good physical, emotional, mental, and spiritual health. Firm pressure is applied by the fingers to specific points, which are referred to as trigger, potent, or acupoints. A practitioner may also use hands, elbows, or feet. This pressure frees tension in the muscles and aids the flow of blood and energy. Endorphins are released, which are neurotransmitters involved in the reduction of pain.

Acupressure is often referred to as acupuncture without needles and is ideal for those who prefer a less-invasive approach.

## Acupuncture

Acupuncture uses very fine needles on specific points throughout the body, known as acupoints. Each relates to an area or function of the body. Depending on the symptoms, needles are inserted into one or several parts of the body and at different depths, then left for short periods of time. Acupuncture is used to relieve pain or dis-ease, as well as to maintain health and well-being, by restoring the natural flow and balance of energy, or chi. Most find the process pain-free.

Acupuncture originates from Traditional Chinese Medicine (TCM), which is based on the principle that good physical, emotional, mental, and spiritual health comes from free and balanced energy within the body.

## Affirmations/Positive Thinking

*The Power of Positive Thinking*: written by Dr. Norman Vincent Peale in 1952, was a groundbreaking, faith-based book on self-improvement. It emphasized replacing negative thoughts and replacing them with positive ones.

In 1976, Louise Hay developed a process of repeating positive statements aloud and coined the term "affirmations". An ongoing practice of repeating affirmations starts a process of change, helps uplift, and encourages on physical, mental, and/or emotional levels. It is more powerful if they are spoken aloud and/or in front of a mirror. The affirmation is always expressed in the present tense, using positive words, and spoken as if it has already happened.

Affirmations are based on the theory that the mind and body cannot differentiate between real and imagined thoughts. As a result of repetition and focus, the positive qualities of these statements become embedded.

An offshoot is afformations, which pose the statement as a question to make it more believable. Instead of "I am happy", it becomes "Why am I happy?".

## Akashic Records

The Akashic Records are a virtual, non-physical library that holds the records of every person's past, present, and future lives.

These records contain details of successful past learning, topics to be revisited, and those yet to be studied. It has details of all the soul contracts that have been made and their status.

Accessing your Akashic Records can bring insight into your purpose, why things happen in this life, and how to best move forward so that the issue is fully completed.

Ancient Indian sages believed in a book recording the details of every soul. The Bible refers to a book containing a record for everyone. Sightings of the Akashic Records have been reported in many near-death experiences. Here, the person is shown significant information.

# Angels

The word angel means "messenger of God." The messages delivered are seen, heard, or known. Many religions speak of angels helping individuals and humanity. There are archangels, guardian angels, angels for specific needs, and so on, who are always available to give guidance and answers. Each has a quality and an area of expertise, although interpretations may vary.

Connecting with angels is as easy as meditating, praying, or talking, although they may come to you at any time. The more time spent developing a relationship with angels, the easier it will become to connect. Communicating is very personal and depends on your beliefs and interests.

The angelic realm can also be accessed through books, oracle cards, and angel healing modalities.

## Aromatherapy/Essential Oils

Aromatherapy balances and promotes harmony of body, mind, and spirit, using aromatic oils extracted from plants. Each one contains beneficial properties and has recommended uses, some of which have scientific validation.

Essential oils are diluted with a carrier oil when used in massage. They may be added to bathwater for absorption through the skin (the largest organ of the body). An infuser or vaporizer fills a whole room with the aroma and qualities of the chosen oil(s).

Natural and nontoxic on the skin, they are not for internal use (unless advised by a qualified practitioner). Certain oils are contraindicated during pregnancy.

The name aromatherapy was first used in 1937 by a French parfumier: however, aromas were used in the ancient civilizations of China, India, Egypt, and possibly even earlier.

## Astrology

Western astrology assists in self-understanding according to the position of the sun, moon, and planets at the exact time, date, and place of birth. A birth, or natal, chart consists of a circle with twelve equal segments, or houses each representing a sign of the zodiac and an area of life. Astrologers interpret each of these in relation to the overall impact of the chart. A deeper reading may include transiting planets sun, moon, which indicate significant dates or changes in direction.

Astro-cartography (location astrology) draws information from the natal chart and a map of the earth. A reading includes advice on the impact of various locations and recommend sand recommends ideal places for an individual or family to live.

Other types of astrology include Eastern or Vedic astrology (Jyoti), which calculates the position of the planets differently than the Western system does. Chinese astrology features animals and employs the lunar, rather than the solar calendar. Lesser-known types of astrology are Tibetan, esoteric, karmic, horary, and soul astrology.

## Ayurveda

Ayurveda is an ancient Indian complementary health system that categorizes people according to the elements, known as the tridosha. Linked to each dosha are conditions, foods, herbs, and activities.

Vata types are often small framed and subject to anxiety and fear. Pitta types are medium build, experience body heat, and are prone to fiery responses like anger. Kapha types have a strong, solid body, with a tendency to be slow and steady. Each person is made up of differing proportions of the tridosha, with one usually dominant.

During a consultation, practitioners will consider all aspects of the client. The pulse is taken to aid diagnosis and advice is given to alleviate symptoms. It may include lifestyle changes, herbs and dietary recommendations.

## Color

Each color has its own wavelength, energy, and feeling. Interpretations are available detailing the energetic qualities and how they change the energy field.

The positive aspects of color can be absorbed by the eyes and/or the skin. You may wear a specific color, meditate on it, or incorporate it into the home or the workplace through decor, pictures, flowers, and plants. Another way is by introducing or increasing color into the diet. There are no rules. Experiment to find what works for you.

As a therapy, colored lights are positioned directly above the skin at specific points on the meridian lines similar to acupuncture, but without needles. Devices that produce color are available for use at home and are supplied with detailed instructions.

## Crystals/Gemstones

Each crystal and gemstone holds and transmits a specific frequency that has been mapped to various positive qualities. These energies can be absorbed, whether they are held, carried on the body, placed in water, or used as a meditation tool. Specific crystals balance many things including the detrimental effects of electronic devices.

The energy can be amplified by placing a number of similar or different crystals in a shape, referred to as a grid.

In a crystal healing session, a therapist selects appropriate crystals and places them on the client. The energy field emitted interacts with the human energy, and the body begins to match this frequency.

## Dowsing

The term dowsing is often associated with a pendulum, although its original meaning referred to a forked stick to detect water. It was held forward and followed as it moved left or right. The stick dropped down to indicate the presence of water.

Dowsing rods are still used for this purpose, as well as in locating oil. Manufactured rods are now available. One of their many uses is to determine the size of an energy field. Some of the energies commonly measured are the aura, crystals, and electromagnetic devices. (Wi-Fi, phone, and electrical wires).

## Dream Interpretation

Dreams are symbolic and offer a doorway into the world of the unconscious mind. This allows an opportunity to process events and emotions that have not yet been resolved. Although there has been interest in dreams and their meanings for thousands of years, a standardized way for interpreting individual dreams has so far not been validated. Each dream is dependent on the individual's interpretation of the symbols.

Analysis is available from mental health professionals and from therapists who specialize in interpreting dreams and using them for healing.

## Family Constellations

Family Constellations explore and unravel hidden and/or unconscious family and ancestral patterns, dynamics, and dysfunctions, which are affecting current life and/or relationships. This is then restructured to bring about deeper understanding, insight, and healing.

Sessions can be either group or individual. In a group, another person energetically represents the family member (who can be living or dead). Each surrogate tunes in to the energy of the character represented. There can be many characters. In an individual session, a placeholder is used to represent another person.

A facilitator leads the session, guiding, prompting, and asking questions as needed. This may culminate in an *a-ha* moment, a revelation, or a deep sense of peace, which may be experienced energetically, visually, kinesthetically, and/or intuitively.

## Feng Shui

Feng Shui (fung shway) recognizes the close relationship between well-being, home and work environments. It eliminates harmful energetic impacts in order to optimize health, well-being, comfort, and happiness.

The floor plan of a property can be divided into nine categories using an octagon-shaped map called a bagua. Remarkable, positive impacts are possible in all areas of life when using this bagua, a compass, the birth date, awareness of the five elemental forces, and Feng Shui principles of interion design.

Feng Shui has been around for more that four thousand years. It has been rediscovered in the past decade or so, with internationally renowned interior designers, architects, and landscapers adopting its precepts in their work.

## Flower Essences

The energetic vibrations of flowers can be imprinted into water and preserved in alcohol as flower essences. They can be taken orally in water or absorbed through the skin. Each flower has a unique vibration and property with which the body is able to come into resonance and harmony.

The characteristics of flowers were known and used in all ancient civilizations, at a time when the link between nature and human health was widely accepted. Like many other ancient systems, this knowledge became largely forgotten.

In the 1930s, Dr. Edward Bach was one of the first to link certain human behaviors with that of specific flowers. The Bach Flower Remedies are still available today. A myriad of flower essences has since been developed (e.g. Australian Bush Flower Essences, Bailey Flower Essences, California Flower Essences, etc.).

# Herbs

Herbs contain phytochemicals (plant chemicals), which are absorbed into the body via the digestion process. Each has been related to the physical body and its various organs and systems. Herbs may be made into a tea or taken in the form of a capsule (the latter is more popular because of the frequently strong and unappetizing taste). Today's agricultural methods, lifestyle, and prevalence of exclusion diets (such as dairy-free or gluten-free) can make it difficult to consume all the nutrients required, and herbs can be useful to address any deficiencies.

All ancient cultures used plants for health purposes. Traditional Chinese Medicine (TCM) and Ayurveda continue to prescribe herbs for their energetic properties to bring the body into health and wellbeing. Herbs are now also being used by some naturopathic doctors and herbalists/herbal practitioners.

Although many now consider herbs to be safer than conventional medicines, it is important to consult your medical practitioner prior to use, as some may interfere with prescription drugs.

Hemp oil is derived from cannabis. It contains cannabidiol (non-psychotropic) and very low or no THC. It is now legal in some countries, sometimes as a dietary supplement, or as CBD oil. It is essential to check the legal status in your country and state of residence before considering taking this.

## Homeopathy

Classical homeopathy is an alternative health system established by Dr. Samuel Hahnemann (1755—1843). It restores healthy balance to the whole person at a physical, emotional, and psychological level.

The underlying principle is that "like cures like." A homeopathic remedy—when given to a healthy person—produces similar symptoms to those of the disease in question. This stimulates the immune system to remove the layers of dis-ease to restore well-being. The layers are removed in the reverse order that they established themselves.

Classical homeopathy prescribes one remedy at a time. The homeopath carefully monitors the patient to see whether the remedy needs repetition, and/or when a new remedy picture occurs.

**The long-term benefit of homeopathy to the patient is that it not only alleviates the presenting symptoms, but it reestablishes internal order at the deepest levels and thereby provides a lasting cure.**

—George Vithoulkas,
International Academy of Classical Homeopathy

## Hypnosis

Hypnosis induces a deep state of wakeful relaxation in a client. In this altered state of being it is possible to access information in the subconscious mind. While focusing on the voice of the therapist, the client is open to the suggestion of new ways of behaving. This reprograms and changes unhelpful or unwanted behaviors, such as smoking.

Hypnosis has been used for millennia. However, it was in the eighteenth century that Franz Mesmer started the process of understanding its scientific principles.

## Kinesiology

Kinesiology (muscle testing) is a diagnostic tool. In the presence of a positive stimuli, muscles strengthen (yes), indicating energy is flowing freely. A weak muscular response (no) occurs with a negative trigger of blocked energy.

Kinesiology is a stand-alone practice. During the consultation, the practitioner will ask various questions and, depending on the muscular response (yes or no) select an appropriate action to restore energy flow.

It is also widely utilized in other modalities for diagnosis, including nutritional therapy, essences, allergy testing, and some forms of healing.

Incorporating principles from Traditional Chinese Medicine (TCM), modern kinesiology has been developed since the 1900s by a succession of chiropractors and scientists who discovered and brought together knowledge about energy flow within the body, the brain, and the nervous system.

## Magnet Healing

The magnetic field of a therapeutic magnet increases blood flow by relaxing capillary walls. This facilitates the distribution of oxygen, nutrients, hormones, and endorphins, which may reduce pain.

There is medical research (Tufts University School of Medicine, New York Medical College, and Baylor College of Medicine) validating use of therapeutic magnets for pain relief. Transcranial Magnetic Stimulation (TMS) has been found to benefit some who experience migraines.

Magnets have been used for healing since 2500—2000 BCE; however, there may be contra-indications, and it is essential to first check with your doctor.

Therapeutic magnets are available for self-healing. We recommend that you receive training or advice, and research thoroughly prior to purchasing or using a therapeutic magnet.

# Meditation

Meditation is simply noticing the mind and any thoughts that are present. Rather than trying to empty or still the mind, observe and allow thoughts, but without getting caught up in a story or judging yourself. When the mind (inevitably) wanders, gently bring it back to the now. This enables the energy behind the thoughts to flow. The nature of the mind is to think. Offering it an alternative focus is helpful for many.

Meditation offers a possibility of coming to a quiet, still space, however fleeting, where new insight and understanding may arise. It has a positive impact on physical, emotional, and mental levels.

Many religions practice meditation, yet meditation is not a religion. There are numerous styles and traditions; however, there is no right or perfect one. Experiment to find a technique that suits you. Do you prefer group practice, using an app, or meditating alone?

# Numerology 1-9

Each letter of the alphabet is given a number 1 through 9. Starting with the letter A, each letter of a person's name (first, middle, last) are added and then the total is reduced by addition to give a single number between 1 through 9. Each number has a specific meaning.

The system works equally well with any alphabet. There are various calculations to add depth: for example, add all vowels in the name (or all consonants or vowels plus consonants). Adding the numbers of the birth date provides an overview—a life umber. Any numbers that are not present in a name highlight areas for learning.

Numerology charts are available online and in many books for self-calculation and meaning. Numerologists also provide this information and give explanations of the numbers.

# Nutritional Therapy

Nutritional therapy is a client based, holistic approach to health and well-being, respecting an individual's unique needs and how these change, depending on age, stage, and lifestyle.

With the increase in stress, toxins, and exclusion diets (e.g., vegan, dairy-free, and/or gluten-free), it is especially important to ensure that the body is receiving all its nutritional needs.

A therapist will advise and identify any nutritional imbalances, pathogens, or negative impacts from environmental factors. The therapist will also assess whether the body is able to digest and absorb nutrients. Diet and lifestyle changes, herbs, dietary supplements, further tests, and well-being practices are suggested to maintain or return to health.

Ongoing scientific research continues to validate the positive effect of a healthy diet in maintaining and restoring health at all levels.

## Past Life

Belief in past lives is widely acknowledged in the East, although it is less so in the West. The underlying principle is that we have lived many lives and reincarnated into different bodies (male and female), families, times, locations, etc. Cases of young children giving vivid accounts of their past lives appear fairly regularly in the media, although most children have little or no recollection. Pay attention to comments that children make before 5 years old.

Knowledge of past-life influences can assist the process of understanding unexplained and unresolved current life challenges. It may clarify why a person has an aversion or fear that is excessive and without reason, or why a person has a natural gift.

Past-life regression brings awareness to past-life issues, which enables the healing process to begin. Many other healing methods can also access and clear these energies.

## Pendulum

The pendulum is a tool to discover information by answering specific questions. It will indicate yes/no/maybe answer in response to a question. If there are many possibilities, the pendulum can be suspended above a chart showing all options, and it will indicate an answer. Various healing methods incorporate a pendulum to facilitate diagnosis and treatment at an energetic level.

A pendulum may be crystal, metal, wood, stone, etc. It will have a chain six to ten inches long, generally a pointed tip and a small sphere or decorative object on the opposite end.

## Pranic Healing

In India, prana is the Sanskrit term for life-force energy, which is also known as chi, or qi, in the Chinese language. pranic healing was developed by Choa Kok Sui (1952-2007) It is a hands-off form of energy healing that affects the energy body, or aura, rather than the physical body.

The energy body is closely linked to the physical body: any changes that happen in in one will automatically affect the other. Keeping the energy body clear and charged with positive energy allows the physical body to do the same. This helps maintain health and well-being.

The physical body is naturally self-healing. In the event of challenges at a physical level, it is able to utilize energy from a healthy, fully charged energy body and then naturally return to optimal health.

## Prayer

Since the dawn of time, humans have looked for help and advice from outside themselves: to nature, the stars and planets, deities and God. This acceptance of something more powerful than the human self and conversing with it, is considered prayer.

Prayer is the earliest form of intention setting and manifestation. It can be an informal conversation or follow faith-specific practices.

> **Studies have shown prayer can prevent people from getting sick—and when they do get sick, prayer can help them get better faster.**
>
> —Harold G. Koenig, MD, Duke University

## Pyramid Energy

Built on principles of sacred geometry and numerology, pyramids amplify unseen energy. There is great significance in the size of the angles. The specific angles of the pyramids at Giza may promote sleep and youthfulness.

The same energetic benefits are available from a pyramid of any size and in any location. To receive the energy, place objects inside, meditate or sleep in one. Archeologists have discovered food, preserved for thousands of years, inside pyramids.

Much Russian scientific research has taken place on seventy-degree-angle pyramids. The conclusion shows that they amplify the energy of physical objects, such as water, flour, medicines, etc.

Pyramid models can be made from various materials (copper, PVC pipe, etc.). They are also available for purchase.

## Reflexology

Reflexology promotes health and well-being by massage of the hand, the ear, and, primarily, the foot. The sole has between one hundred thousand and two hundred thousand nerve endings, making reflexology highly effective for calming the nervous system. Reflexology reduces stress and anxiety creating a state of relaxation.

Each part of the foot, hand, and ear are mapped to a part of the body and/or an organ. During a treatment, practitioners detect areas of the body where there are challenges and/or bring awareness to potential problems.

Many find this a gentle and very relaxing experience, as if the whole body is gently massaged.

Reflexology originates from Traditional Chinese Medicine (TCM), which dates back many millennia.

## Reiki

Reiki (ray-key) is a Japanese word that means **universal life-force energy**—an energy that is all around us and present in all living things. Reiki is a natural, holistic way to bring about physical, mental, and emotional well-being. If life-force energy is low, the body is more prone to stress and sickness if it is high, the body is more likely to be healthy.

Reiki practitioners are attuned to this eergy and chanel it through their hands to the recipient. They will gently place their hands on or just above the client's body at specific points, which activates the body's own natural ability to heal itself.

Lost for centuries, Reiki was rediscovered, channeled, and taught by Dr. Mikao Usui. New developments include reiki Drumming, Angel Reiki, and Holy Fire Reiki.

## Runes

Runes are a set of stones that are interpreted for insight into questions, scenarios, and possible outcomes. There are sets of between twenty-four and thirty-three stones. Each stone has a meaning and shows a symbol from the ancient runic alphabet of Northern Europe.

Readings may be based on one stone or more. Stones may also be placed in set patterns, which add deeper meaning and significance.

The word rune means letter, mystery, or whispered secret. The history is uncertain, but it has links to Norse mythology and the Vikings.

# Sacred Geometry

Sacred geometry consists of various shapes that form the foundation of the universe. These shapes include the circle, triangle, square, pentagon, hexagon, heptagon, and octagon. Examples in nature are petals, tree branches, nautilus shells, crystals, stars, galaxies, DNA, and the cornea of the eye. Most are seen within the Flower of Life (shape), which is found all over the world.

One or more mathematical principles—phi, pi, the golden ratio, and the Fibonacci sequence, etc.—are hidden within all sacred geometry. Each shape has its own specific vibration and acts as a doorway to a different energetic frequency.

The energies of sacred geometry can be accessed by meditation, visualization, images, objects, or by focusing on one of the many ancient architectural sites built on its principles, such as the pyramids at Giza (Egypt), and Stonehenge (England).

# Shadow Work®

We all have a shadow part of us, a dark side, an aspect of which we are not proud—or possibly not even aware of. Often hidden, shut off, and ignored, it is completely subconscious and unknown. Discovering, acknowledging, and integrating the shadow side brings about self-acceptance and peace.

Originating in ancient shamanic teachings, the shadow became part of Western psychology. Ancient and modern ideas were synthesized in the Shadow Work modality by Cliff Barry in 1988. In Shadow Work, the group and facilitators create a safe space where the shadow can be explored, expressed, seen, and heard. This enables deep transformation.

## Shamanic Healing

Shamanic healing harnesses the power of the earth and world of spirit.. the shamanic healer will first create sacred space and then enteran altered state of consciousness, through the use of drumming, chanting, or medicinal hers. Moving between the worlds of living and dead, they may access ancestral, current, or past lives—wherever the root of dis-ease and blocked energy resides.

Shamans are assisted by power animals and spirit guides. Their many tools include the medicine wheel, sage, drums, rattles, voice, journeying, vision quests, and soul retrieval.

Every ancient civilization had a form of shamanism. These were the medicine people, healers, and sages.

## Sound Healing

Every organ and part of the body as an optimal frequency. Sound healing retunes the body by playing the appropriate frequency so that it can return to alignment, health, and well-being.

Sound healing tools include the voice (singing, chanting, toning) and instruments (gongs, crystal bowls, drums, bells, tuning forks). Sessions can be individual or in groups—sound meditation, drumming, circle, gong bath/gong meditation.

Music is available at specific frequencies for health and well-being. Each is mapped to a variety of positive qualities. These vibrations may be based on ancient frequencies: for example, solfeggio (do--re-mi-fa-so-la-ti) or other models. Binaural beats, listened to through headphones, play different tones in each ear, and the attunement takes place at the frequency difference.

BioAcoustics analyzes the voice to detect missing frequencies which can then be listened to, enabling the body to return to harmony.

## Tarot/Oracle Cards

Tarot is a card-based system that gives information and insight to a question of significance. Each card represents certain characteristics and possibilities, which are further developed by its position in the spread, telling a story and providing insight that many find to be uncannily accurate.

Developed in the late eighteenth century, the tarot deck consisted of seventy-eight cards with images. They included the major arcana of twenty-two cards and the minor arcana, which had four suits: wands, swords, cups, and pentacles. Although nowadays there are many types of designs and themes, the deck is largely unchanged.

**Oracle cards** are free from the structure of tarot. They may show words or phrases, as well as images. The number of cards in an oracle deck varies widely. Each set of cards has a theme: angels, animals, archetypes, flowers, sacred geometry, etc.

## Touch for Health®

Touch for Health® Kinesiology (TFHK) combines muscle testing, acupressure, touch, and massage. The session starts with a consultation and setting of a goal. Using muscle testing as a biofeedback mechanism, the therapist will assess how the energy flows in relation to the goal. Muscles show a strong response to positive stimuli and free-flowing energy. A weak muscular response occurs with a negative trigger or blocked energy. Massage helps to release energy blockages.

# Traditional Chinese Medicine (TCM)

Traditional Chinese Medicine (TCM) maintains and restores health and well-being by bringing the body's energy systems into balance—internally, externally, and with its environment.

The energy is called qu, or chi, and flows through meridians, which can become blocked, creating imbalance in the body, The twelve main meridians are linked to physical and emotional characteristics, specific organs, emotion, and one of five elements (wood, fire, earth, metal, water).

A TCM practitioner makes recommendations to restore balance in the body. These may include foods, herbal remedies, acupuncture, acupressure, shiatsu massage, reflexology or activities (e.g. tai chi, qi gong, and nei gong).

# Vibrational Essences

Vibrational essences contain an energetic frequency that is imprinted into water and preserved in alcohol. Everything is energy and, therefore the vibration and properties of any object may be channeled into an essence. The energies of places, crystals, angels, and healing frequencies have all been included in essences.

Introducing these positive energies enables the body to vibrate at a frequency higher than the negative energies of fear, stress, and anxiety. This gives the body an opportunity to come into resonance, balance, and harmony.

Vibrational essences are an extension of flower essences. They can be taken orally in water or absorbed through the skin. Essences are available that include color, plant, and crystal energies (Aura Soma Essences, etc.)

# PART 8

# HEALING WITH THE BODY

The body is a highly effective instrument for changing how your feel and restoring the natural flow of energy. It can provide an amazingly powerful way to access and clear challenges, especially those related to events and emotions beyond conscious memory.

The body is our vehicle for life; it holds our history, our loves, and our fears. The more awareness we have, the more free our energy will be, and the easier our journey will become.

## Dance

Free-form dance is a wonderful way to let the body move as it needs to, without any restriction, and to get in touch with what is going on right now. Join a group, or dance at home when you have a few minutes. Groups have some structure, guidance, and sharing, but there are no steps to learn. You may dance alone, with another, or as a group. The energies and rhythms invite the body to communicate and move from deep within. There are many to choose from, including 5Rhythm, Biodanza, Chakra Dancing, and Qoya.

## Grounding/Earthing

Grounding, or earthing is connecting with the earth via the skin. This simple, free, and highly effective technique includes walking barefoot and/or touching the ground, trees, rocks, etc. Many benefits are reported: improved sleep and health, reduced pain and stress symptoms, and many others. Schumann resonance, or the vibration of the earth, is said to be the frequency of well-being for humans. You may have experienced this during your childhood, when spending time barefoot, at the beach, or in nature.

## Massage

Massage combines the healing effect of touch and the movement of energy to release physical tightness, pain, discomfort, and energetic blocks, creating a feeling of well-being. Therapists use oil and their hands to rub, knead, pummel, or palpate the body. The NO-HANDS massage technique uses the forearms and body weight.

Many styles of massage are available, ranging from gentle touch, to sports and deep-tissue massage. Depending on the type of massage, essential oils, hot stones, lava shells, or suction cups may also be utilized. Massage dates back to ancient China and Greece, prior to 2000 BCE.

## Osho Active Meditations

Osho developed meditations in a way never seen before. These meditations include moving, shaking, vocalizing, and letting go. At some point, stillness is also part of the process. These meditations are usually practiced in groups, often very large ones. The energy and noise build and build, with a great stirring—bringing insight and release.

> **Real meditation means: don't avoid the inner madhouse; enter into it, face it, encounter it, be watchful, because it is through watchfulness that you will overcome it.**
>
> —Osho, The Secret of Secrets

## Qigong/Tai Chi

Qigong (chi gong) combines gentle meditative movements and breathing to mobilize and strengthen the body. It helps the energy flow to restore or maintain well-being on a physical, emotional, and energetic level.

Qigong originated in China around 5000 BCE. Tai Chi (tie chee) developed later and is sometimes referred to as the martial-art form of qigong. Like all martial arts, it uses energy rather than body strength.

## Rolfing® Structural Integration

Rolfing® is a hands-on deep-tissue manipulation of the facia muscles, ligaments, and tendons; it aims to balance the body, reduce pain, and optimize alignment and posture. It comprises a series of ten sessions that treat the etire body structure.

Sessions start with a mobility assessment, followed by bodywork. This includes getting up from the table and walking around during the session so that the therapist can assess and review the client's progress. Clients usually work in their underwear.

Rolfing® was developed by American Biochemist Dr. Ida Rolf (1896-1970).

## Shiatsu

Shiatsu is a non-invasive, hands-on bodywork that adjusts the body and balances energy flow. Sessions include massage, rotation of joints, and application of pressure to one or more of the six-hundred acupressure points in the body. Therapists may use their fingers, thumbs, elbows, knees, and sometimes feet. Clients lie on a mat on the floor and wear light clothing.

Shiatsu originated in Japan around 1900 and has its origins in Traditional Chinese Medicine (TCM).

## Somatic Experiencing®

Somatic Experiencing® is a safe and gentle practice that gradually releases trauma from the body. It is based on the principles discovered by Peter Levine. He noticed that although animals run or shake to discharge shock and trauma, humans do not. These energies often become stuck, resulting in physical, mental, psychological, and emotional stress and tension, which impede the joy of life.

The main priority is to ensure that the client is not re-traumatized. Clients are helped to feel safe and develop resources to support them during the session. The somatic process of being with, feeling, and vocalizing the sensations in the body starts the process of shifting the energy gently and at the client's pace, as both body and nervous system relax.

The client may sit or lie and remains fully clothed. There is no touch by the practitioner.

## Tantric and Sexual Healing

We all have sexual energy, and just like any other energy, it needs to be acknowledged, respected, and allowed to flow. Blockages occur by societal conditioning, trauma, and negative experiences (medical issues, invasive surgeries, violence, abuse, self-judgment, phobias, addictions, etc.).

Tantra and Tao have established energy practices to cultivate and increase life-force/sexual energies and to restore energy flow and health. Many other systems are becoming available, and these also offer support to bring sexual energies into harmony. They may help with fertility, confidence, boundaries, sexuality, intimacy, all of which in turn lead to the creation of healthy relationships.

Some examples of this type of specialist massage are the Arvigo Techniques of Maya Abdominal Therapy® (external), Holistic Pelvic Care™ (internal), and Tantric Journey (external and internal). Sexual bodywork sessions include Nirvana™, Body Dearmouring, and Sexological Bodywork™.

Therapists are highly respectful and boundedaried, and they follow a strict code of conduct.

## Yoga

Yoga unites and aligns physical, energetic, mental, emotional, and spiritual levels. The goal is to bring you to a mediative, calm state of oneness, with the potential for reflection, understanding, and insight into all aspects of life.

Yoga has been practiced for more than five-thousand years and has a wealth of information on philosophy and psychology. However, the postures practiced today are a much more recent addition.

Postures (asanas) develop and maintain a strong healthy body. They may be physically challenging, very gentle, or somewhere in between. Sessions can also include breathing (pranayama), chanting a mantra, and/or using a hand position known as a mudra—all of which have positive energic vibrations. It is possible to have a deep energetic and emotional release while holding a posture or during meditation.

Although many groups now focus on the body and postures only, the Yoga Sutra, which dates back more that two-thousand years (prior to that, it was an oral tradition), lists postures as one aspect of an eight-step process that culminates in deep meditation leading to Self-realization.

There are numerous styles and traditions, group classes, one-on-one sessions, and yoga therapy for those with specific challenges and/or interests. No one method is right or better; each has its own attributes. Explore and research to find what suits you best, and consider trying several different styles.

# PART 9

# CONCLUSION

Many believe that we are in the process of a new paradigm shift, the birthing of a new world view. Quantum physics is bringing understanding to the world of energy. Documented evidence is now proving that thoughts, feelings, and emotions affect the body chemistry. The electro-magnetic field of the heart changes according to whether it experiences love or fear. This science-based knowledge is evolving and becoming known to a growing audience.

Trained scientists—Dr. Bruce Lipton and Gregg Braden, to name just two—are speaking and writing in a way that is accessible to many, unifying science with ancient knowledge and spirituality. It takes time for new ways to become mainstream, yet we believe they will.

These discoveries, although considered "new", are actually new only to today's world of science. Many ancient civilizations understood and foretold things that were outside our comprehension until recently, or were dismissed as primitive, particularly by the Western world.

Links are now being made to the power of the inner world and how it relates to the body and daiy life. There is a remembering, or a re-awakening, in tandem with the scientific paradigm shift, of the possibility and potential we each have by using our own inner world.

A growing body of information and research is available. However, the world of energy and healing can be used *now*, without the necessity of understanding the science. Your feelings, thoughts, and emotions affect what happens in your body and your daily experiences. This understanding can have a profoundly positive effect on your life. Simply be aware and cultivate all things positive.

You are permanently connected with the world of the invisible, subconscious, and unknown. Your tools to interact with it are the four I's—*instinct, intention, intuition, and imagination*—and the Clairs, which include clairvoyance (seeing with the "mind's eye"), *clairaudience* (an inner hearing of information), *claircognizance* (an inner knowing beyond doubt), and *clairsentience* (an inner feeling bringing forth insight and knowledge).

Although not yet widely acknowledged, these are powerful tools that provide information and insight beyond the conscious mind, leading to new possibilities and potential.

**The doorway is always open.**

Healing is wholeness. It is a place of observing or witnessing the ups and downs of life (present or past events), neither getting drawn into dramas, reactions, blaming, and judging, nor swept away by agitation, upset, and emotional turmoil. Healing can take place at the physical, emotional, mental, psychological, and spiritual levels.

There is much healing that can be done alone, whether with a personal development approach or self-use of one of the many modalities in this book. However, there are often times when input from a practitioner is valuable. This can be in the form of life understanding readings, coaching/counseling, experiential workshops, learning a technique, or receiving a session. Choices include using a newer, lesser-known technique, or one that is established and more mainstream.

Healing can be accessed via the body, and this is especially helpful for clearing trauma and pre-verbal events. Whatever technique is chosen, it is important to support the body with nutrition and bodywork. This ensures the energy is flowing and balanced.

It may appear that there are many choices; yet, while researching different methods of healing, we have been reminded of the similarly between all modalities, both old and new, even though they are presented in different ways. The underlying difference is the energy frequency o the modality, the frequency of a practitioner (in that moment), and the practitioner's self-knowledge.

Flip through this book, look at the table of contents, and review the resources section. Be open to clues and messages in your daily life, and synchronicities, leaflets, or adds that appear. Your inner world of insight and intuition will guide you.

As we have said, there is no right or better modality. Choose whichever one(s) you are drawn to; whatever feel drawn to will be what you need at that time: Your frequency changes when healing occurs. This ripples out into the world, and it is your contribution to the paradigm shift.

**Changing your vibration changes the world.**

# PART 10

# RESOURCES

## Part 2 An Invisible World

### The Invisible World
https://lonerwolf.com/things-we-cant-see/
https://www.greggbraden.com/
http://www.dailymail.co.uk/sciencetech/article-5161615/Physicists-say-theyve-confirmed-new-form-matter.html
http:/www.superconsciousness.com/topics/environment/can-plants-read-our-thoughts

Baugh, John, PhD. Before You Know It: 770 Unconscious Reasons We Do What We Do. New York: Touchstone, an imprint of Simon & Schuster, © 2017

Emoto, Masaru. lie Hidden Messages in Water. Translated by David A. 'Thayne. New York: Atria Books, © 2001

Lipton, Bruce H. The Biology of Belief: Unleashing the Power of Consciousness. Matter & Miracles. London: Hay House UK, © 2015

### Instinct
https://www.ifaw.org/journal/incredible-animal-instincts
https://sites.google.com/site/lifesciencesinmaine/15-behavior-of-animals
https://www.goodreads.com/quotes/tag/instinct
https://www. meriam-webster.com/dictionary/instinct

https://www.quora.com/What-are-some-examples-of-instinctive-behaior-in-humans-and-animals

## Intention

https://www.drwaynedyer.com/press/power-intention/
https://www.thebalance.com/inspirational-quotes-for-work-about-iintuition-1918441
https://www.empowering-personal-development.com/power-of-intention.html
https://positivepsychology.com
www.meriam-webster.com/dictionary/intention

Dyer, Wayne W. *The Power of Intention: Learning to Cocreate Your World Your Way.* Carlsbad, CA.., Hay House, © 2004

Martin, Dianne. *The Book of Intentions.* Hillsboro, OR: Beyond Words Publishing, © 2002

McTaggart, Lynne. *Intention Experiment: Use Your Thoughts to Change the World.* London: Harper Element, an imprint of Harper Collins, © 2007, 2008

## Intuition

https:/www.psychologytoday.com/blog/here-there-and-everywhere/201205/20-quotes-intuition
https://www.psychologytoday.com/blog/the-intuitive-compass/201108/ what-is-intuition-and-how-do-we-use-it
http://operationmeditation.com/discover/what-is-intuitionsix-points-to-ponder/
http://www.huffingtonpost.com/2014/03/19/the-habits-of-highly-in_tu-n_4985788.html
www.merriam-webster.com/dictionary/intuition

Choquette, Sonia. *Tune In: Let Your Intuition Guide You to Fulfillment and Flow.* Carlsbad, CA: Hay House, © 2011, 2013

Dale, Cyndi. The Intuition Guidebook: *How to Safely and Wisely* **use your sixth sense**. Minneapolis, MN: Deeper Well Publishing, © 2011

Day, Laura. *Practical Intuition: How to Harness the Power of Your Instinct and Make It Work for You*. New York: Villard Books, a division of Random House, © 1996.

Kahneman, Daniel. *Map of Bounded Rationality: A Perspective on Intuitive Judgment and Choice*. Prize Lecture, Dec. 8, 2002

## Imagination

http://awakenthegreatnesswithin.com/50-inspirational-quotes-on-the-power-of-your/imagination/
https://www.ryuc.info/creativityphysics/mind/imagination_key_cration.htm
www.twainquotes.com

## Channeling

Ce Anne: www.visionarhguidance.com/
Forever Conscious: http://foreverconscious.com
LeeCarroll: http://www.kryon.com/About_Kryon.html
Lee Harris: http://www.leeharrisenergy.com
Steve Rother: https://www.espavo.org

Roman, Sanaya; Packer, Duane. *Opening to Channel: How to Connect with Your Guide*. Tiiburon, CA: H. J. Kramer Inc. © 1987

## Miscellaneous

Alper, Frank, Dr. *Our Existence Is Mind: Healing Methods for the Third Millennium*. Hergiswil NW Switzerland edition ADAMIS, reissued 2016

—*Universal Laws for the Aquarian Age*. Phoenix, AZ: Arizona Metaphysical Society, © 1986

Brennan, Barbara Ann. *Hands of Light: A Guide to Healing through the Human Energy Field*. New York: Bantam Books, a division of Bantam Doubleday Dell Publishing Group, Inc., © 1988

—*Light Emerging: The Journey of Personal Healing.* New York: Bantam Books: © 1993

—*Core Light Healing.* Carlsbad, CA: Hay House, Inc., © 2017

Goleman, Daniel. *Emotional Intelligence: Why It Can Matter More Than IQ.* New York: Bantam Books, © 1995

Lakhiani, Vishen. *The Code of the Extraordinary Mind.* New York: Rodale Wellness, Inc., © 2016

McTaggart, Lynne. *The Field*. London: Element, an Imprint of Harper Collins Publisher, © 2001

Pert, Candice B., PHD. *Molecules of Emotion: Why You Feel the way You Feel.* London: Scribner, 1997; London: Simon & Schuster UK Ltd., 1998; Pocket Books, © 1999

Tolle, Eckhart. *A New Earth: Awakening to Your Life's Purpose.* London: Penguin Books Ltd., © 2005

## Part 4 Kick-starting Your Healing: Changing Your Thinking

**Forgiveness**

https://www.virtuesforlife.com/forgiveness/

Holub, Ana. *Forgive and Be Free: A step-by-Step to Release, Healing & higher Consciousness.* Woodbury, MN: Llewellyn Publications. © 2016

**Gratitude**

https://greatergood.Berkeley.edu/article/why_gratidude_works
https://positivepsyhologyprogram.com/category/gratitude/
https://positivepsychologyprogram.com;gratt7de-appreciation
https://www.nytimes.com/2015/11/22/opinion/sunday/choose-to-be-grateful-it-will-make-you-happier.html
www.dailygood.org/story/532/how-gratitude-can-help-you-through-hard-times-robert-emmons

**Love**
Khan, Matt. *Whatever Arises LOVE That*. Boulder, CO. Sounds True, © 2016

# Part 6: 21st Century Healing Modalities: A Selection of Innovative New Techniques

## Anusha Healing
http://www.anushahealing.co.uk/

Hayes, Patsi. Anusha *Rising: A Pathway to Healing and ascension to Higher Dimensions*. London: Live It Publishing. © 2017

## Biological Decoding®, TotalBiology® Biodecoding®
http://bouron.net/bioreprogramming.net/bioreprogramming
htttp;//bouron.net/
http://bioreprogramming.net/about isabelle
https://catherinesilver.com/mind-body-connection/

Benarous, Isabelle. *Break the Code of Your Illness: The Link Between Emotional Distress and Health Disorders*. Los Angeles, CA; Bioreprogram ming® Press, © )2010

Bouron, Enrique. *Decodificatacion Microbiologicia Y Vir*al. Kier, © 2013 (in Spanish)

## Celebration of Being/Relationships
https://www.celebrationofbeing.co.uk/
http://www.corexperience.com

## Eden Energy Medicine
Eden, Donna; with Feinstein, David, PhD. *Energy Medicine: Balancing Your Body's Energies for Optimal Health, Joy and Vitality*. New York: Jeremy P. Tarcher/Penguin, a member of Penguin Group, © 1998, 2008

Eden, Donna with Feinstein, David, PhD. Energy Medicine for Women: *Aligning Your Body's Energies to Boost Your Health and Vitality.* New York: Jeremy P. Tarcher/Penguin, a member of Penguin Group, © 2008

## Emotional Freedom Technique (EFT)
https://www.palace of possibilities.com/post/30-eft-tapping
https://www.thetappingsolution.com/what-is-eft-tapping/
www.EFTUniverse.com

Ortner, Nick. *The Tapping Solution. A revolutionary System for Stress-Free Living.* Carlsbad, CA: Hay House Inc. © 2013
—*The Tapping Solution for Pain Relief*: *A step-by-Step guide to Reducing and Eliminating Chronic Pain.* Carlsbad, CA. Hay House Publishing, © 2015
—*The Tapping Solution for Manifesting Your Greatest Self: 21 Days to Releasing Self-Doubt, Cultivating Inner Peace, and Creating a Life.* Carlsbad, CA: Hay House Publishing, © 2017

## Energy in Motion (EMO)
https://goe.ac/what_is_emetrance.htm

Hartmann, Silvia. *EMO Energy in Motion.* © 2017

## Men's Groups/Community Groups
https://mankindproject.org/
https://www.illuman.org/
http://aband of brothers.org.uk/
http://www. aabandofbrothers.org/
http://wwwmalejourney.org.uk/
http://www.malejourney.org.uk/
http://menscraft.org.uk/

## Metatronic Healing®
www.metatronic-life.com

Merivale, Philippa. *Rescued by Angels*. Ripley Hants, England: O Books, John Hunt Publishing, Ltd, © 2004

—*77% Wizdom of Oz*. Ripley Hants, England: O Books, John Hunt Publishing, Ltd, © 2010

—*Harps of Gold: Healing Beyond Time and Space*. Charleston SC: Create Space, © 2011

## Quantum Touch®
https://quantumtouch.com/

Gordon, Richard. *Quantum Touch: The Power to Heal*. Berkeley, CA: North Atlantic Books, © 1999, 2002, 2006

—*The Secret Nature of Matter*. Berkeley, CA: New Atlantic Books, © 2017

—; Duffeld, Chris, PhD, Wickhorst, Vickie, PhD. *Quantum-Touch 2.0: Discovering and Becoming*. Berkeley, CA: North Atlantic Books, © 2013

Herriott, Alain. *Supercharging Quantum Touch: Advanced Techniques*. Berkeley, CA: North Atlantic Books, © 2007

Herriott, Alain, Herriott, Jody. *Quantum Touch: Core Transformation: A new Way to Heal and Alter Reality*. Berkeley, CA: North Atlantic Books, © 2009

## ReconnectiveHealing®/TheReconnection®
www.thereconnection.com

Pearl, Eric, Dr. *The Reconnection: Heal Others, Heal Yourself*. Carlsbad CA: Hay House Inc., © 2001

Pearl, Eric, Dr., Ponzlov, Frederick. *Solomon Speaks on Reconnecting Your Life*. Carlsbad, CA. Hay Hoouse Inc., © 2013

**The Body Code®**
http://bodycodehealingsystem.com/

**The Emotion Code®**
https://www.www.healerslibrary.com/heart-wall/
http://www.drbradleynelson.com

Nelson, Bradley, Dr. *The Emotion Code: how to Release Your Trapped Emotions for Abundant Health, Love and Happiness*. Mesquite, NV: Wellness Unmasked Publishing, © 2007

**Theta Healing ™, (Theta Healing®, ThetaHealers®)**
https://thetahealing.com/about-thetahealing.html

Stibal, Vianna. *ThetaHealing™; Introducing an Extraordinary Energy-Healing Modality*. Carlsbad A: Hay House, Inc., © 2006, 2010
—*Advanced* ThetaHealing™; Harnessing the Power of All That Is. Carlsbad, CA: Hay House, Inc.., © 2008, 2011
—*ThetaHealing™: Disease and Disorder*. Ammon, ID: Rolling Thunder Publishing, © 2008

**Women's Circles/Community Groups**
https://awakeningwomen.com/womens-temple/
content/uploads/2014/03/Guidelines-in-How-to-Form-a-
http://redtenttemplemovement.com/ www.wombblessing.com/

# Part 7: Established Healing Modalities: Pre-Twenty-First-Century Healing

**Acupressure**
http://www.acupressure.com
https://acupuncture.org.uk/about-acupuncture/

Gach, Michael Reed. *Acupressure.* London: Judy Piakus (Publishers) Ltd., ©1992

Houston, F. M., D.C., D. D., PhD. *Healing Benefits of Acupressure: Acupuncture without Needles.* 2nd ed. New Canaan, CT: Keets Publishing, Inc., © 1991

## Acupuncture

http://www.medicalacupuncture.org/For-Patients/Acupuncture-in-the-News
www.acupuncture.org.uk
www.acupuncture-points.org
www.acupuncturetoday.com/abc/
https://acupuncture.org.uk/about-acupuncture/
www.acupuncture.org.uk

## Affirmations/Positive Thinking

www.louise hay.com/affirmations

Myers, Pam: Worth, Sally. *Rekindled Ancient Wisdom Affirmations,* Book 1. Revised and Expanded, 3rd edn. Rutherford, NSW, 2320, Australia Ancient Perceptions, © 2009

## Akashic Records

www.edgarcayce.org/the-readings/akashic-records/

Barnett, Lis. *The Infinite Wisdom of the Akashic Records.* Hamton Plains, NJ: New Page books, a division of the Career Press, Inc. © 2015

Howe, Linda. *Healing through the Akashic Records: Using the Power of Your Sacred Wounds to Discover Your Soul's Perfection.* Boulder, CO: Sounds True, © 2011

Muranyi, Monika. *The Human Akash: A Discovery of the Blueprint Within.* Outremont, Quebec, Canada: Ariane Books, © 2014

Zortiz, Ernesto. *The Akashic Records: Sacred Exploration of Your Soul's Journey within the Wisdom of the Collective Consciousness.* Hampton Plains, NJ: New Page Books, a division of The Career Press, Inc. © 2015

Smith, Jacki; Shaw, Patty. *Do It Yourself Akashic Wisdom: Access the Library of Your Soul.* San Francisco, CA. and Newburyport, MA: Weiser Books, © 2013

## Angels
www.crystalinks.com/angels

Alexandria, Chris. *Pick-a-WooWoo: Have You Ever Wondered About Angels?* Pick-a-Woo Woo Publishers: Weiser Books, © 2013

Colton, Ann Ree and Murro, Jonathan. *Galaxy Gate: Vol. 11 The Angel Kingdom.* Glendale, CA: Ann Ree Colton Foundation, © 1984

Cortens, Theolyn. *Working with Archangels: A Path to Transformation and Power.* London: Piatkus Books, Ltd., © 2007

Gregg, Susan. *The Encyclopedia of Angels, Spirit Guides, &Ascended Masters: A Guide to 200 Celestial Beings to Help, Heal, and Assist You in Everyday Life.* Beverly, MA: Fair Winds Press, © 2009

Lysette, Chantel. *The Angel Code: Your Interactive Guide to Angelic Communication.* Woodbury, MN: Llewellyn Publications, © 2010

Nahmad, Claire. *In the Arms ofAngels: Messagesfrom the Angelic Realms to Help You on Your Way.* London: Watkins Publishing, © 2012

Newhouse, Flower A. *The Kingdom ofthe Shining Ones.* Escondido, CA: The Christward Ministry, 1955

Raven, Hazel. *The Angel Bible: The Definitive Guide to Angel Wisdom.* New York, New York; London: Sterling Publishing, © 2006

Solara. *Invoking Your Celestial Guardians.* 2nd edn. Mt. Shasta, CA: StarBorne Unlimited, © 1987

Virtue, Doreen. PhD. *Archangels & Ascended Masters: a Guide to working and Healing with Divinities and Deities*. Carlsbad, CA: Hay House Inc., © 2003

Virtue, Doreen, *Angel Numbers 101: The Meaning of 111, 123, 444, and Other Number Sequ*ences. Carlsbad, A: Hay House Inc. © 2008

**Aromatherapy/Essential Oils**
http://naha/explore-aromatheraphy/about-aromatherapy/
www.organicfacts.net/health-benefits/essential-oils

Cohen, Jody. Heal the Body, *5 Steps to Calm Anxiety, Sleep Better, and Reduce Inflammation to Regain Control of Your Health.* TenSpeadPress.: ©2021

Rose, Jeanne. *The Aromatherapy Book: Applications & Inhalations.* Herbal Studies Course. Jeanne Rose: San Francisco, A: Hay House Inc. Berkeley, CA: North Atlantic Books, © 1992

Watson, Franzesca. *Aromatherapy Blends and Remedies.* London, San Francisco, CA: Thorsons, an imprint of Harper Collins Publishers, © 1995

Worwood Susan. *Essential Aromatherapy: A Pocket Guide to Essential Oils and Aromatherapy.* San Rafael, CA: New World Library, © 1995

Worwood, Valerie Ann. *The Complete Book of Essential Oils and Aromatherapy.* Sann Rafael, CA: New World Library, (C) 1991

Zielinsky, Eric; Sabrina Ann Zielinsky. *The Essential Apothecary: Advanced Strategies and Protocols for Chronic Diseases and Conditions.* Rhodale Books © 2021

**Astrology**
https://www.astrologers.comabouthistory/
https://www.vijayajyoti.com/what-is-jyotish/
http://www.astro.com/astrology/in_vedic3_e.hrm
http://astrocartography.co.uk/ACG.htm

http://astrostyle.com/learn-astrology/the-12-zodiac-houses/
www.chinahightlghts.com/travel guide/hinese-zodiac/
www.elsaelsa.com www.KeplerCollege.org

Lewi, Grant. *Heaven Knows What*. St. Paul, MN: Llewellyn Publications, © 1970

McEvers, Joan. *12 Times 12: 144 Sun/Ascendant Combinations*. San Diego, CA: ACS Publications, Inc., © 1983

Oken, Alan. *Soul-Centered Astrology: A Key to Your Expanding Self Freedom*, CA: The Crossing Press, © 1990

Spiller, Jan. *Astrology for the Soul*. New York: Bantam Dell, a division of Random House, Inc., © 1997

## Ayurveda
http://www.ayurvedahealth.org/aboutayurveda.htm
www.ayurveda.com/blog
www.experiencelife.com/ayurveda
www.nccih.nih.gov/health/Ayurveda/introduction.htm

Lad, Vassant. *Ayurveda: The Science of Self-Healing*. Twin Lakes, WI: Lotus Press, a division of Lotus Brands, © 1994

## Chakras
https://www.the-energy-healing-site.com/chakras.html
http://www.alchemyrealm.com/chakras.htm

See amazon or any retailer for many good books on chakras

## Color
https://www.visualmedicine.org/
http://chromalighttherapy.com./inyto.html
www.therapycolor.co

Dinshaw, Darius, *Let There Be Light*. Malaga, NJ: Dinshaw Health Society, © 1985

Gimbbel, Theo. DCE, MIACrT, NFSH, Cert. Ed. Form, *Sound, and Healing*. Essex, England: C. W. Daniel Co. Ltd. (©) 1987

Luscher, Max, Dr. tr. and ed. By Scott, Ian. *The Luscher Color Test*. New York: Random House, © 1969

## Crystals

https://crystalvaults.com
https://healing-crystals-for-you.com
https://meanings.crystalsandjewelry.com

Calverley, Roger. The *Language of Crystals*. Toronto, Ontario, Canada: Radionics Research Association, © 1986

David, Judithann H., Van Hulle, JP. *Michael's Gemstone Dictionary*. Orinda, Ca: Affinity Press, © 1990

Hall, Judy. *The Crystal Bible*: A Definitive Guide to Crystals. Cincinnati, OH: Walking Stich Press. © 2003

—*The Crystal Bible 2*. Cincinnati, OH: Walking Stich Press, © 2009

Mottana, Annibale: Crespi, Rodolfo, Giuseppe Liborio. Prinz, Maretin: Harlow, George; Peters, Joseph; eds. (The American Museum of Natural History). *Simon & Schuster's Guide to Rocks and Minerals*. New York: A Fireside Book, Simon & Shuster, Inc., © 1977, 1978

Richardson, Wally; Richardson, Jenny; Huett, Lenora. *Spiritual Value of Gem Stones*. Marina del Rey, CA: DeVorss & Company, © 1980

## Dowsing

https://dowsers.orks//
http://www.britishdowsers.org/

Cowan, David & Cowan, Erina. *Dowsing Beyond Duality*: Access *Your Power to Create Positive Change.* San Francisco, CA; Newburyport MA: Weiser Books., 2012

## Dream Interpretation

https://www.psychologytoday.com/blog/out-the-ooze/201801/the-freudian-symbolism-in-your-dreams

http://time.com//dream-therapy-sleep/4737463

www.psychologytoday.com/blog/dream-catcher/201703/dream-interpretation

## Family Constellations

https://realacademy.net/daan-van-kampenhout

https://constellationintensive.com/daan-von-kampenhout/

https://www.thecsc.net/

https://www.hellinger.com/en/family-constellations/

https:www.verywellmind.com/what-is-famiily-constellation-therapy-5217964

https://ifs-institute.com

Manné, Joy, PhD. *Family Constellations: A Practical Guide to Uncovering the Origins of Family Conflict*. Berkeley, CA: North Atlantic Books, © 2009

Preiss, Indra Torsten. Tr. From Dutch. *Family Constellations Revealed: Hellinger's Family & Other Constellations Revealed (7he Systemic View)*. Antwerp, Belgium. North Charleston, SC: CreateSpace Independent Publishing Platform, © 2012

Wolynn, Mark. *It Didn't Start with You. How Inherited Family Trauma Shapes Who We Are & How to End the Cycle*. New York, New York: Penguin Boos, an imprint of Penguin Random House, LLC, © 2016

*End the Cycle*. Penguin Books, animprint of Penguin Random House © 2016

## Feng Shui

https://www.carolehyder.com/general/

https://ifsguild.org/feng-shui-blog/

http://www.dummies.com/health/understanding-the-principles-of-feng-shui
http://www.vaastuinternational.com/fengshui.html

Carter, Karen Rauch. *Move your Stuff, Change Your Life: How to Use Feng Shui to get Love, Money, Respect and happiness.* New York: fireside Books, a division of Simon & Schuster, © 2000

Hyder, Carole J. *Wind & Water: Your Personal Feng Shui Journey.* Minneapolis, MN: Hyden Enterprises, © 1998, 2008

Kuok, Man-ho. *The Feng Shui Kit: The Chinese Way to Health, Wealth, and Happiness at Home and at Work.* Boston, MA: Turtle Publishers, an imprint of Periplus Editions (UK), © 1995

Too, Lillian. Easy-to-Use-Feng-Shui. London: Collins & Brown Ltd. © 1999

Sang, Larry Master. Translated and co-written by Luk, Helen. *The Principles of FENG SHUI.* Monterey Park, A.: The American Feng Shui Institute, © 1994

## Flower Essences

http://www.flowersociety.org/flower-gallery/flower-photo-gallery.htm#
https://www.onegardenessences.com/history-of-flower-essences.html

Gurudas (Channeled through Kevin Ryerson). *Flower Essences and Vibrational Healing.* Albuquerque, NM: Brotherhood of Life, Inc., © 1983

Hynde-Jones, T. W. *Dictionary of the Bach Flower Remedies[TM]: Positive and Negative Aspects.* Saffron Walden, Essex, England: The C. W. Daniel Company Ltd., © 1976

## Galactic Healing

Kaehr, Shelley, PhD. *Galactic Healing.* Dallas, Tx.: An Out of%is World Production, © 2003

## Herbs

https://nccih.nih.gov/health/herbsataglance.htm
https://danusirishherbgarden.com/
https://www.americanherbalistsguild.com/herbal-medicinefundamentals
http://www.dailymail.co.uk/health/article-5175825/Medical-marijuana-NO-public-health-risks-declares.html
http:/www.dailymail.co.uk/health/article-5174379/Cannabis-prevent-mental-decline-HIV-sufferers.html /
http://www.livinggrass.primemybody.com/home/

Carse, Mary, M.N.I.M.H. *Herbs of the Earth: A Self-Teaching Guide to Healing Remedies.* Hinesburg, VT: Upper Access Publishers, © 1998

Christopher, John R. Dr. *School of Natural Healing.* Springville, UT. Christopher Publications, Inc., © 1976

Grieve, Mrs. M. F.H.S. *A modern Herbal.* 1st published by Johnatan Cape Ltd., 1931; 2nd revised edn., 1973, 3rd by Crosset Press: London: imprint of Random Century Group. Dorset Press, a division of Marboro Books Corp., © 1992

Mercola, Joseph. *Effortless Healing: 9 simple Ways to Sidestep Illness, Shed Excess Weight and Help Your Body Fix Itself.* London: Hay House, © 2015

Santillo, Humbart, B.S., M. H. *Natural healing with Herbs.* Prescott Valley, AZ: Home Press, © 1987

Smyth, Angela. The Complete home Healer: Your Guide to Every Treatment for Over 300 of the Most Common Health Problems. New Your San Francisco, CA: a division of Harper Collins Publishers, © 1994

Tierra, Michael, C.A., N.D. Supplemented by Dr. David Frawley, OMD, and Christopher Hobbs. Planetary *Herbology An Intergration of Western Herbs into the Traditional Chinese and Ayurvedic Sy*stems. Santa Fe, NM: Lotus Press, © 1988

—*The Way of Herbs*. New York: Pocket Gooks, a division of Simon & Schuster Inc., © 1990

Werner, David; with Thuan, Carol, Maxwell, Jane. rev. ed. *Where There is No Doctor: A Village Health Handbook*. Berkeley, Ca: The Hesperian Health Guides, (C) 1992

Willard, Terry, PhD. *The Wild Rose Scientific Herbal*. Calgary, Alberta, Canada: Wild Rose College of Natural Healing Ltd., © 1991

William, Anthony, *Medical Medium: Secrets Behind Chronic ad Mystery Illness and How to Finally Heal*. Carlsbad, CA: Hay House, Inc., © 2015

—*Medical Medium: Life-Changing Foods: Save Yourself and the Ones You Love with the Hidden Healing Powers of Fruits & Vegetables*. Carlsbad, CA: Hay House Inc. © 2016

—Medical Medium: Thyroid Healing: The Truth Behind Hashimoto's, Grave's, Insomnia, Hypothyroidism, Thyroid Nodules & Epstein-Barr. Carlsbad, Ca.: Hay House, Inc.,© 2017

—Medical Medium: *Liver Rescue*, plus others

## Homeopathy

https://www.vithoulkas.com/homeopathy/about-homeopathy
http://homeopathyeurope.org/homeopathy/
www.homeopathycenter.org/getting-started-homeopathy
www.homeopathyusa.org
https://www.hri-research.org/

Fry, Kathleen K. MC, CTHHom. *"What's the Remedy for That?" The Definitive Homeopathy Guide to Mastering Everyday Self Care without Drugs*, Collette Avenue Press, ©2017

Patel, Aarti, N.D. *Picture It: Homeopathy: A Picture-Based Guide to Homeopathic Remedies and Personalities*. CreateSpace Independent Publishing Platform, © 2012

## Human Design

Bunnell, Lynda with Hu, Ra Uru. *The Definitive Book of Human Design. The Science of Differentiation*. Carlsbad, CA: HDC Publishing, © 2011

Curry, Karen. *Understanding Human Design: The New Science of Astrology: Discover Who You Really Are*. San Antonio, TX: Hierophant Publishing, © 2013

Hu Ra Uru. *The Complete Rave I'Ching: Gates, Lines, Positions, Themes, rosses, Commentaries*. Santa Fe, NM. Human Design America. © 2000

Rudd, Richard. Circuitry: *A Complete guide to Circuits, Channels & Gates*. Santa Fe, NM: Human Design America, 2005

—*Gene Keys: Unblocking the Highest Purpose Hidden in Your DNA*. New York, New York: Warner Books edn. By arrangement with Harper & Row, Publishers, Inc., © 2009

## Hypnosis

https//hypnosis.edu/hypnotized
http://www. aaph.org/hypnosis-FAQ
www/historyofhypnosis.org

## Inner Child

https://ppsychcentral.com/blog/6-steps-to-help-heal-your-inner-child
www.indful.org/healing-thechild-within/the-inner-child

## Kinesiology

http://www.oneillcolege.com.au/history-of-kinesiology/

Diamond, John, M.D. *Your Body Doesn't Lie-How to Increase Your Energy Through Behavioral Kinesiology*. New York. Warner Books, by arrangement with Harper & Row Publishers, Inc., © 1978

## Magnet Healing

https://www.livescience.com/1410174-magnetic-therapy.html
https://www.mayoclinic.org/tests-proceedures/transcranial/

magnetic-stimulation/about/pac-20384625
https://www.spineuniverse.com/treatments/magnet-therapy

Davis, Albert R.; Rawles, Walter C. *Magnetism and Its Effects on the Living System*. New York: Exposition Press, © 1975

Meyers Bryant A. M.A, *Physics. PEMF: The Fifth Element of Health*. Bloomington, IN: Balboa Press, a division of Hay House, © 2014

Null, Gary, PhD. *Healing with Magnets*. New York: Carroll & Graf edn. A division of Avalon Publishers, inc. © 1998

Payne Buryl, PhD. Healing: *Advanced Techniques for* the *Application of Magnetic Forces*. Two Lakes, WI: Lotus Press, © 1997

—*The Body Magnetic*. Rev. ed., Soquel, CA: PsychoPhysics Press © 1992

Philpott, William; Kalita, Dwight K.; Lothrop, Linwood. *Magnet Theory: An Alternative Medicine Definitive Guide*. Garden City Park, New York: Square One Publishers, 2012

Tierra, Michael, OMD. *Biomagnetics and Herbal Therapy*. Twin Lakes WI: Lotus Press, © 1997

**Meditation**
http://anericanmeditationsociety.org/meditation/benefits/

**Numerology 1 to 9**
https://www.numerology.com/about-numerology/articles/what-is-numeology/
http://nameprofiler.azurewebsites.net/language=eng

Buess; Lynn M. *Numerology for the New Age*. Marina del Reu, CA: DeVorss & Company, © 1989

Bunker, Dusty. *Numerology and Your Future*. Atglen, PA: Whitford Press, a division of Schiffer Publishing. Ltd., © 1980

Campbell, Florence, M.A. *Your Days Are Numbered: A Manual of Numerology for Everybody*. Ferndale, PA: The Gateway, © 1931 (renewed in 1958, 19th ed. © 1976

Connolly, Eilene. *The Connolly Book of Numbers: Vol. I: New Path to Ancient Wisdom. The Fundamentals*. North Hollywood, CA: Newcastle Publishing Co., Inc., © 1988

—*The Connolly Book of Numbers: Vol II: A New Path to Ancient Wisdom*: The Consultant's Manual. North Hollywood, CA: Newcastle Publishing Co., Inc., © 1988

Javane, Faith. *Master Numbers: Cycles of Divine Order*. Arglen, Pa: Whitford Press, a division of Schiffer Publishing, Ltd., ©1988

—; Bunker, Dusty. *Numerology and the Divine Triangle*. Rockport, MA: Para Research, © 1979

Kryder, Rowena Partee. *Destiny: Gaia Matrix Oracle Numerology*. Mount Shasta, CA: Golden Point Productions, © 1995

Marsdon, Blue. *Soul Plans: Reconnectr with Your True Life Purpose*. London; Hay House, U.K., Ltd., © 2013

Millman, Dan. *The Life You Were Born to Live: A Guide to Finding Your Life Purpose*. Tiburon CA: H.J.Kramer Inc., © 1993

Ngan, Nicholas David. *Your Soul Contract Decoded: Discovering the Spiritual Map of Your Life with Numerology*. London: Watkins Publishing, © 2013

Pither, Steven Scott. *The Complete Book of Numbers: The Power of Number Symbols to Shape Reality*. St. Paul, MN: Llewellyn Publications, © 2002

Young, Ellin Dodge. *You Are Your First Name*. New York: A Long Shadow Book, Pocket Books, a division of Simon & Schuster, © 1983

**Nutritional Therapy**
https://nutrition.org/publications/
https://hydrationhttps://www.danusirishherbgarden.com.comfoundation.org/
http://bant.org.uk/about-nutritional-therapy/bant-wellbeing-guidelines/
http://www.vrg.org/nutrition/

Carlson, Wade. *Eat Away Illness: How to Age-Proof Your Body with Antioxidant Foods*. West Nyack, NY: Parker Publishing co., © 1986

Cohen, Dana, Bria, Gina. *Quench: Beat Fatigue, Drop Weight, and Heal Your Body Through the New Science of Optimum Hydration*. Hachete Books. © 2018

D'Adamo, Peter J., Dr.; with Whitney, Catherine. *Eat Right 4 Your Type: The Individualized Diet Solution to Staying Healthy, Living Longer & Achieving Your Ideal Weight*. New York G. P. Putnam's Sons, © 1996

Grotto, David, RD, ND. 101 Foods That Could Save Your Life. New York: Bantamdell, a division of Random House Inc., © 2007

Lutz, Carroll A., M.A. RN; Przytulski, Karen Rutherford, M. S., RD. *Nutritional and Diet Therapy*. Philadelphia, PA: F.A. Davis Co., © 1994

Murray, Michael T., N. D. *The Healing Power of Foods: Nutrition Secrets for Vibrant Health and Long Life*. Rocklin, CA: Prima Publishing, © 1992

Ni, Maoshing, PhD., C.A.; with McNease, Cathy, B.S., M.H. *Tao of Nutrition*. 2$^{nd}$ edn. Santa Monica, CA: Seven Star Communications, © 1994

Powell, Tag, Dr., and Powell, Judith. *Taming the Wild Pendulum: Make Decisions and Solve Problems with This Unique Psychic Tool!* Pinellas Park, FL: Top of the Mountain Publishing, © 1995

Alberto Villoldo. *Grow a New Body: How Spirit and Power Plant Nutrients Can Transform Your Health*. Hay House. © 2019

Wolcott. William; Fahey, Trish. *The Metabolic Typing Diet*. New York: Broadway Books, © 2000

## Past Life

https:/lonerwolf.com/past-lives—soul-reincarnated/
https://www.edgarayce.org/about-us/blog/blog-categors/reincarnation/
https//crystalinks.com/reincarnation.html

Colton Ann Ree, *Draughts of Remembrance: Memories of Past* Lives. 2$^{nd}$ ed., Glendale, CA: Ann Ree Colton Foundation of Niscience, Inc., © 1956, 1959

Lane, Barbara. *16 clues to Your Past Lives: A Guide to Discovering Who You Were.* Virginia Beach, VA: A.R.E. Press, © 1999

## Pendulum
www.crystalinks.com/pendulums

Chandu, Jack E. *The Pendulum Book.* Essex, England: C.W. Daniels Ltd., © 1990
Conway DJ. *A Little Book of Pendulum Magic.* New York: Crossing Press Random House, Inc © 2001
Jurriaanse, D. *The Practical Pendulum Book.* First published (in Dutch) © 1984, Holland; York Beach, ME: Samuel Weiser, Inc., © 1986
Olson, Dale W. *The Pendulum Bridge to Infinite Knowing: Beginning Through Advanced Instruction Complete with Pendulum Charts.* Eugene, OR: Crystalline Publications, © 2011
Powell, Tag, Dr., and Powell, Judith. *Taming the Wild Pendulum: Make Decisions and Solve Problems with This Unique Psychic* Tool! Pinellas Park, Fl., Top of the Mountain Publishing, © 1995

## Pranic Healing
http://pranichealing.com/

## Prayer
https://www.crosswalk.com/faith/prayer/prayers/23-short-prayers.html
https://www.goodreads.com/quotes/tag/prayer

## Pyramid Energy
http://healingenergytools.com/pyramid-work

Gaunt, Bonnie. *The Stones Cry Out.* Self-published. © 1991
Osmanagich, Sam, Dr. Sci. *Pyramids Around the World & Lost Pyramids of Bosnia.* "Archeological Park: Bosnian Pyramid of the Sun" Foundation. © 2012

### Reflexology
www.mayoclinic.org/healthy-lifestyle/consumer-health/expert-answers/ what-is-reflexology/faq-20058139

### Reiki
https://iarp.org:learn-about-reiki/

### Runes
tttps:///norse-mythology.org/runes/
http://www.crystalinks.com/runes.html

### Sacred Geometry
http://www.ancient-wisdom.com/sacredgeometry.htm
www.crystalinks.com/sg.html

Linn, Donna. *Beyond the Code*. Lettra Press © 2025
Lundy, Miranda. *Sacred Geometry*. New York: Walker & Co., © 2001
Mitchell, John; with Browne, Allan. *How the World Is Made. The Story of Creation According to Sacred Geometry*. Rochester, VT: Inner Traditions, © 2009
Olson, Scott. *The Golden Section: Nature's Greatest Secret*. New York: Walker & Co., © 2006
Skinner, Stephen. *Sacred Geometry: Deciphering the Code*. New York: Sterling Publ. Co., © 2006

### ShadowWork®
Bly, Richard. *The Little Book of the Human Shadow*. New York: Harper Collins, (1998)

### Shamanic Healing
https://shamaniceducation.org/what-is-a-shamanic-healing/
www.firechild-designs.co.uk/healing.html

Ingerman, Sandra. *Shamanic Journeying: A Beginner's Guide*. Boulder, CO: Sounds True, Inc., © 2004

## Sound Healing
https://www.healingsounds.com/articles-and-interviews/
https://www.musictherapy.org/about/
http://wholetones.com/wholetones

Goldman, Joshua; Sims, Alec W. *Sound Healing for Beginners*. Woodbury, MN: Llewellyn Publications, © 2015
McKusick, Eileen Day. *Tuning the Human Biofield*. Rochester, VT: Healing Arts Press, © 2014
Tyrrell, Michael S. *The Sound of Healing: Unveiling the Phenomena of Wholetone*s. Brandon, SD: Barton Publishing, © 2015

## Tarot/Oracle Cards
https://science.howstuffworks.com/science-vs-myth/etrasensory-perceotuibs.tarot-card/htm
https://www.tarot.com/tarot/cards/major-arcana
https://www.tarot.com/tarot/cards/minor arcana
http://www.ata-tarot.com/reflections/
www.daily-tarot-girl.com

Greer, Mary K. *Tarot for your Self: A Workbook for Personal Transformation*. 2$^{nd}$ edn. Franklin Lakes, NJ. The Career Press, Inc. a division of New Page Books, © 2002
Katz, Marcus; Goodwin, Tali, *Around the Tarot in 78 Days: A Personal Journey Through the Cards*. Woodbury, MNL Llewellyn Publishers, © 2012
Katz, Marcus. *Tarosophy® Tarot to Engage Life, Not Escape It*. Salamander and Sons. © 2001, 2015, 2016

## Touch for Health(R)
http://www.touch4/health.com/about.houc-fir-health

## Traditional Chinee Medicine (TCM)

https://www.temworld.org/what-is-tcm/
https://www.tcmworld.org/what-is-tcm/five-elements
http://www.shen-nong.com

Tierra, Leslie, L.Ac., Herbalist. *The Herbs of Life: Health and Healing Using Western & Chinese Techniques.* Freedom, CA: The Crossing Press, © 1992

Tierra, Dr. Michael, L.Ac., OMD, A.H.G.: Tierra Leslie, L.Ac.A.H.G. *Chinese Traditional Herbal Medicine Vol. 1: Diagnosis and Treatment.* Twin Lakes, WI, Lotus Press, © 1998)

## Vaastu

http://www.vaastuinternation.com/vaastu_blogs/vaastu_blogs.html

## Vibrational Essences

https://www.bfvea.com/resources/BFVEA.com/about-essences/
https://oshadhi.co.uk/
https://vtblueoils.com

Gurudas. *Gem Elixirs and Vibrational Healing.* Vol. II. Boulder, C0: Cassandra Press, © 1986

Hynde-Jones, T.W. *Dictionary of the Bach Flower Remedies™: Positive and Negative Aspects.* Saffron Walden, Essex, England: The C.W. Daniel Company Ltd., © 1976

# Part 8: Healing with the Body

## Arvigo®

https://arvigotherapy.com

## Biodanza

https://www.biodanzaassociation.uk/

http://biodanzawestlondon.com/about-biodanza/
www.biodanza.us/

**Body Dearmouring**
https://tantricbodywork.co.uk/what-is-de-armouring/

**5Rhythms Dance**
https:///www.5rhythms.com/

Roth, Gabrielle. *Sweat Your Prayers: Movement as a Spiritual Practice*. Dublin, Ireland: Gill & Macmillan. Ltd. With associated companies through the world. © 1999

**Holistic Pelvic Care™**
http://www.wildfeminine.com/

**Massage**
https://www.amtamassage.org/research/Massage-Therapy-Research-Roundup.html
http://www.massagetherapy.com/learnmore/benefits.php
www.mayoclinic.org/healthy-lifestyle/stress-management/in-depth/massage/art-20045743

**Nitvana™ Bodywork**
http://www.sashacobra.com

**Osho Active Meditations**
http://www.osho.com/meditate/active-meditations/dynamic-meditation

**Qigong/Tai Chi**
http://www.energyarts.com/what-qigong
http://www.taichinews.com/about-qigong
http://www.taichiunion.com/what-is-tai-chi-chuan/

## Rolfing® Structural Integration
https://www.rolf.org https://www.rolfinguk.co.uk/

## Sexological Bodywork™
https://seologicalbodyworkers.org/what-is/

## Shiatsu
http://www.acuprressure.com/applshiatsu_theapy.htm
http://www.shiatsusociety.org/treatments/about-shiatsu

## Somatic Experiencing®
http://www.sositernational.org/somatic-experienceing-training/

## Tantric and Sexual Healing
https://tantranectar.com/history-of-tantra/
https://www.tantra-essene.com/learning-tantra/what-is-tantra/
https://www.britishmuseum.org/blog/what-is-tantra
http://www.trantricjourney.com/tantric-treatments/

DeVoss, Minke. *Tao tantric Arts for Women: Cultivating Sexual Energy, Love, and Spirit*. VT: Destiny Books. © 2016

Sarita, Mahassatvaa Ma Ananda PhD. Divine Sexuality: *The Joy of Tantra*. Scotland UK: Findhorn Press, © 2003, 2011

Kent, Tami Lynn. *Wild Feminine: Finding Power, Spirit & Joy in the Female Body*. New York: Atria Books; Hillsboro, OR. Beyond Words, © 2011

## Yoga
https://www.viniyoga.com/viniyoga-free-samples/
http://www.layt.org/
https://www.yogastudies.org/dharma-dowloads/

Desikachar, T.K.V. *The Heart of Yoga: Developing a Personal Practice*. Rochester, VT. Inner Traditions International, © 1999

Singleton, Mark. *Yoga Body: The Origins of Modern Posture Practice*. New York: Oxford University Press Inc., © 2010

## Miscellaneous—Quotes

https://chopra.com/articles/5-steps-to-setting-powerful-intentions
https://www.americamagazine.org/content/ignatian-educator/steven-spielberg-listen-whisper
https://www.brainyquote.com/
https://www.goodreads.com/author/quotes/87041.Alan_Turing
http://www.greatest-inspirational-quotes.com/intention-quotes.html
http://www.quotationspage.com/quote/38353.html
http://www.spiritual-quotes-to-live-by.com/neale-donald-walsch.html
www.goodreads.com/quotes
www.quoteland.com

## Miscellaneous—Inspirational Speakers

Byron Katie—http://thework.com/en
Joe Dispenza, Dr.—http://www.drjoedispenza.com
Marianne Williamson—https://marianne.com/
Michael Bernard Beckwith—https://www.michaelbernardbeckwith.com/
Neale Donald Walsh— http://www.nealedonaldwalsch.com/
Gregg Braden— https://greggbraden.com also on you tube
Bruce Lipton—https://www.brucelipton.com also on you tube
Dr. Gabor Mate— https://drgabirmate.com also on you tube

## Miscellaneous—Programs

Heartmath Institute—https://www.heartmath.org
Personal Growth—https://wwww.nubdvakketacadent.com/

## Miscellaneous—Resources

Blackburn Losey, Meg, Dr. *The Children of the Now: Crystalline Children, Indigo Children, Star Kids, Angels on Earth, and the*

*Phenomenon of Transitional Children*. Franklin Lakes, NJ: The Career Press, Inc., © 2006

—*Touching the Light: Healing Body, Mind, and Spirit by Merging with God Consciousness*. San Francisco, CA, Weiser Books an imprint of Red Wheel/Weiser, LLC, © 2011

Brown, Michael. *The Presence Process*. British Columbia, Canada: Namaste Publishing, © 2010

Byrne, Rhonda. *The Secret*. London: Simon & Schuster UK Ltd. © 2006

Carroll, Lee; Tober, Jan. *The Indigo Children: The New Kids Have Arrived*. Carlsbad, CA, CA, Hay House Inc., © 1999

—*An Indigo Celebration*. Carlsbad, CA, Hay House, Inc., © 2001

—*The Indigo Children Ten Years Later. What's Happening with the Indigo Teenagers!* Carlsbad CA: Hay House Inc, © 2009

Jaffe Kabir; Davidson Ritama. *Indigo Adults: Understanding Who You Are and What You Can Become*, Franklin lakes, NK: New Page Books, a division of the Career Press, Inc., © 2009

Loyyd Alexander, PhD, N.D. with Johnson, Ben, MD, DO, NMD. *The Healing Code:6 Minutes to Heal the Source of Your Health, Success, or Relationship Issue*. New York: Grand Central Life & Style, Hachette Book Group, © 2010

Schucman, Helen. Ed. Schucman, Helen; Therford, William T. *Course in Miracles*. Original Edition Text published by Course in Miracles Society, Nebraska: Course in Miracles Society, © 2001

Wilber, Ken; Patten, Terry; Leonard, Adam; Morelli, Marco. *Integral Life Practice: A 21$^{st}$ Century Blueprint for Physica Health, Emotional Balance, Mental Clarity, and Spiritual Awakening*. Boston, MA: Integral Books, an imprint of Shambhala Publications, Inc., © 2008

All Books by Gregg Braden or Dr. Bruce Lipton
https://www.brucelipton.com/books/
https://www.worldofbooks.com/en-gb/collections/author-books-by-gregg-braden

# PART 11

# NEW RESOURCES

Donna or Suzan have direct knowledge of all the modalities showcased in this book—we know the teachers, have taken their classes, have read their books or know friends that are respected healers in their own right that know the other particular modalities.

**In this section** are modalities that have come to our attention since this book was readied for publication, but do not know enough about them at this time to include. We have listed (with websites) those new modalities that have caught our attention, but no direct knowledge.

We have checked most of the web sites in the whole book to see if they are still active. Donna is in the United States and some work only in the U.S.: Suzan is in England and some of the websites work only in that part of the world. And some of the web sites work for both of us!

It is important to **do your own research**—not only for the all modalities listed within the book, but especially for those that are now making their way into awareness. We have attempted to give you clues for that research, but it is not nearly complete.

**Much information** will be found on the internet, podcasts, in newly published books or word of mouth. Check with trusted of friends and/or metaphysical stores which will know many of the new modalities emerging—or know where to find more information on them. But **most of all** check in with your intuition and gut feeling to see if it is right for you.

**Be aware** of the amount of hype and misinformation that may be available for the new modalities. Maybe it is true, or perhaps not as glowing as promised.

**Be discerning**, use your own intuition, ask for guidance from those you trust before committing to ANY modality.

**Be willing** to walk away if it does not "feel" right (i.e., makes you feel uncomfortable in any way).

**Remember, every body reacts differently, and not every modality will give the same effect on each person.** It is learning to trust your body to tell you what it needs—physically, emotionally, mentally, or spiritualy.

**We wish you well on your journey.**

**May you find the information that you need
to transform your life in whatever way you need
for your best and highest good.**

**Astrology**
**Joni Patry,** vedic astrology—podcast, classes

**Body & Breathwork**
https://biodynamicbreath.com/

**Postural Restoration**
https://www.posturalrestoration.com/pri-resources/articles/newspaper-magazine-and-in-service/
https://www.sensingvitality.com/

https://www.mantakchia.com/about-universal-healing-tao/
https://blocktherapy.com

## Diet & Lifestyle as Medicine
https://hydrationfoundation.org/
https://www.danusirishherbgarden.com/
https://nutritionfacts.org/
https://wwvolutionaryherbalism.com/

## Energetics
https://davidrouter.com/about/energy-field-studies/
https://polaraidhealth-global.com/
https://www.kinesiologyassociation.org/

## Energy Healing
Rahani
https://www.rahannicelestialhealing.co.uk/discover-rahanni

## Bioresonance
https://www.bioregmed.com/historybioresonance.html

## Bioenergetic Wellness System – NES
https://www.e4l.com/

## Family Constellations
https://systemic-ritual.com/
https://www.asconstellations.co.uk/freeresources.html

## Frequency healing
Rife Machine -
https://www.researchgate.net/publication/278020661_The_Rife_Handbook_of_Frequ10ncy

Therapy and Holistic Health an integrated approach for cancer and other diseases 5th Edition
https://jwlabs.com/

**Personal Development**
https://theshiftnetwork.com/
https://www.dailyom.com/

**Red Light**
Red light therapy
https://blogs.mercola.com/sites/vitalvotes/archive/2025/01/13/new-study-links-red-light-therapy-to-reduced-clot-risk.aspx
https://www.youtube.com/watch?v=AkvpcziY7GY
https://zeneyeinstitute.com/blog/declining-eyesight-improved-with-red-light-therapy/

**Infra-red sauna**
https://cdn.shopify.com/s/files/1/0610/2204/4352/files/SaunaProtocolsEbook.pdf?v=1712567617

**Sound Healing**
Safe & Sound Protocol
https://integratedlistening.com/products/ssp-safe-sound-protocol/
https://www.healingsounds.com/
https://www.drgemmaperry.com.au/

**Visual Medicine**
https://www.visualmedicine.org/

**Programs/Summits/Webinars**—cutting edge information on various topics
Jonathan Landsman—NaturalHealth365 Programs
Nick Polizzi—Healthy Kitchen

Brian Vaszily—The Art of Anti-Aging
Ari Whitten, M.S.—the energy blueprint

## PODCASTS
https://www.mercola.com/downloads/podcast.htm
https://www.culturedfoodlife.com/cultured-food-life-podcast/
https://vibrantblueoils.com/category/podcast/
https://theenergyblueprint.com/podcast/
https://biologyoftrauma.com/biology-of-trauma-podcast/
https://www.bentinhomassaro.com/podcasts
https://drsvoboda.com/podcast/

BARBARA O'NEIL—Eternal Health
https://www.youtube.com/channel/UCQU6CBip7gR99VlWJ5STvJw

Penny Kelly (intuition and consciousness)
https://rumble.com/c/PennyKelly

Stars Align with Carmen.com (numerology)
Tina Chaudry Astrology

New Thinking Allowed (consciousness and multiple relevant topics)
https://greenmedinfo.com/greenmed/dsplay/disease
https://www.hubermanlab.com/podcast
https://www.mercola.com/downloads/podcasts/htm
https://charleseseinenstein.or/podcasts/
https://biologiyoftrauma.com/biology-of-trauma-podcasts/
https://vibrantblueoils.com/category/podcast/
https://theenergyblueprint.com/podcast/
https://www.intuitivemind.org/blog/
https://www.asconstellations.co.uk/blog
https://greggbraden.com/blog
https://greenmedinfo.com/gmi-blogs

https://drarielleschwartz.com/arielles-blog/
https://sarahmccrum.com/blog/
https://resilienceinformedtherapy.com/blog/
https://www.pruneharris.com/blog
https://blog.energyawareness.org/
https://irenelyon.com/podcast-guest-appearances/
https://klinghardtinstitute.com/category/article/

**Books**

https.com/Essential-Oils-Boost-Brain-Heal/dp/1984858602/ref=sr_1_1?s=books&sr=1-1
https://www.amazon.com/Quench-Fatigue-Through-Science-Hydration-ebook/dp/B0763KGMXW/ref=sr_1_1?s=books&sr=1-1
https://www.amazon.com/Grow-New-Body-Nutrients-Transform/dp/1788172051/ref=tmm_pap_swatch_0?_encoding=UTF8&sr=1-1

**Other Resources**

https://biodynamicbreath.com/
https://www.realhealth-onlibe.com/
https://www.healingsounds.com/

# ACKNOWLEDGMENTS

A big thank you to all our friends who helped and supported us while writing this book. Your love, humor, sharing of knowledge, insight, and expertise have helped in so many ways, and you have made our lives brighter by being in it:

Arthur Graye
Barbara Dancer
Cé Änn
Cheryl-Iya Broadfoot
Crystall Raines Fertel
Dinah Barton
Eloy Machuca
Flavio Cernotta
Jennifer Low
Jenny Jones
Jenny Jury
Joseph ZatKieal Syverson
Lisa Branson
Louise Page
Marilyn Nichols
Mary Kathoryn Syverson
Patsy Hayes
Rachel Whitehead
Susan Harmon
Virginia Stewart

May thanks also to our guest authors for contributing articles.

To all our teachers, past or present, and those we have yet to meet, we give our heartfelt thanks.

To our many students and clients in-person and on-line who have shared the journey with us.

To those who have believed in this book and answered our many, many questions about the publishing process.

# ABOUT THE AUTHORS

## Donna Linn

Donna Linn has had a wide range of interests in the metaphysical field. For more than fifty years, she learned everything she could through classes, books, workshops, and friendships. Donna became more involved in the healing aspect of metaphysics when her husband started actively pursuing and using his innate healing ability.

She and her husband welcomed many people to their metaphysical store (1990—2001). It offered books, crystals, jewelry, healing sessions, sponsored classes, workshops, and speakers. Donna also lectured at many venues about how herbs were used historically.

She continues to study and practice many different modalities, including Astrology, AumaKhua-Ki®, Biological Decoding®, Divine Healing, teacher of Galactic Healing®, Historical uses of Herbs (C.H.). Human Design, teacher of Numerology, Quantum Touch®, Reiki (master teacher), Soul Contract 1 and 2, and Theta Healing ™, among others.

After retiring from public-school teaching, she began writing ad subsequently began to try to publish those books, which are listed below and available from LettraPress

**Breaking the Code** (utilizing date of birth to reveal significant years) –coming soon

**Beyond the Code** (using sacred geometry pictures to receive information and answers to questions asked) Lettra Press 2025

**Inside the Code** (recognizing numerology and pictures with the I Ching matrix) coming next year)

**Searching** with Suzan J Wells (how to use intent, intuition, and imagination to derive answers and information about 70 different ways that the invisible energy flow can be used for healing. Lettra Press, 2025

**Using the Code** (A different way to read a name chart, and ways to find important years in your life with the math already done for you. (coming next year)

Donna continues to teach, write, and share her extensive knowledge of healing and numerology with individuals and groups. She teaches Galactic Healing®, Esoteric Numerology workshops, and also Esoteric Numerology readings, both short and long (in person and on line)

To schedule a Galactic Healing® session or class, an Esoteric Numerology workshop, or an individual Esoteric Numerology reading, contact her at @2donnamessick.com (subject line: numerology)

## Suzan J Wells

One day, Suzan knew beyond doubt that something had to change, that her life could not continue as it was: busy and stressful, always juggling, always putting everyone's needs ahead of hers. It was as though life just happened, and she had no choice or say. She felt a deep yearning for meaning and questioned whether there was more to life.

Things started slowly with yoga, an aura reading, and a self-healing course. Then, in 2010, Suzan had a reading and felt at a deep level that everything had been as it should. There was a plan for her life, and she had made the plan. It dawned on her, in the most profound way, that this meant she could change things. And she has. Many times. Along the way, she experienced feeling lost, directionless, and confused, thinking that the task was impossible.

After more readings, numerous types of healing, and learning that included physiology, psychology, philosophy, of ancient yogis. She studied established and cutting-edge energy techniques, meditation, body, breath and voice practices. There were structured as well as intuitive techniques, leadership skills, and training to teach others, Suzan has given numerous healings, as well as leading groups and workshops for more than twenty years. She has also co-authored this book Decoding Universal Energy and Healing

Suzan's experience has gone from merely existing to being fully present in her body and in the world, enjoying life and living her purpose.

Her deepest desire is to help you find the quickest and easiest possible way to live authentically and to your full potential, and to share the things she wishes she had known earlier.

**Other books written by the author:**

**Breaking the Code: Numerology with a twist**

**Beyond the Code: Energy with Sacred Geometry**

**Inside the Code: Numerology within the I Ching**
Decoding Universal Energy and Healing
- The 4 I's - Healing Methods - Resources

**Using the Code: A Continuation of Beyond the Code Numerology**

www.ingramcontent.com/pod-product-compliance
Lightning Source LLC
Chambersburg PA
CBHW061736070526
44585CB00024B/2691